NAVIGATING

GRIEF

WITH GRACE

PJ Spur

A V E R Y
Publishing

Dedication

This book is dedicated to

My husband Steve

My daughters Meagan and Sara

And my granddaughters Avery and Emersyn

Each one of you brings a smile to my face and
makes my heart sing!

Table of Contents

Cover Art by Artist Paula Mitchell, who creates beautiful art, whether you want a portrait of your children or your favorite pet. www.facebook.com/paulamitchelldesign/

Acknowledgements

In 1999, I was healing from a break-up. I searched on the internet for some form of support and I found Richard Ross, an intuitive counselor who introduced me to EFT (Gary Craig's Emotional Freedom Technique). I started to heal and began studying EFT and applying it to my daily life. Then, I taught it to my daughters, as well.

When I began studying hypnotherapy in 2005, I knew I would incorporate EFT in some way. Later that year, I earned my certificate in EFT and began introducing it to clients, teaching classes and creating tapping scripts. Along the way, I added other energy clearing modalities, crystals and essential oils to my tool kit for personal healing and my work with clients.

Thank you to my darling husband, Steve and his support and encouragement. Because of his dreams in 2001, we stepped on the spiritual path we are navigating today. He keeps me grounded, reminds me to "turn off" after a busy day and gives me Reiki treatments for free!

As he began his work as a Psychic Medium, I began to see that my work would also include supporting others as they grieve. People not only grieve the loss of friends and family members, they also grieve pets, jobs, houses and cities. Yes, grief is a part of life and we heal and grow as we realize this truth and seek support as we grieve.

Along the way, I have learned about meditation and a spiritual approach to living that goes far beyond the religion of my childhood. I hope that some part of what I have learned comes through and comforts you. Please know that the tools and techniques in this book will support you as you honor what you are feeling and begin to release and heal, so you can know peace.

-PJ Spur, February 2016

Section One - Introduction
What is Grief?
Grief…a word that comes from Middle English and Anglo-French roots meaning *an injustice* or *calamity*. Its synonym is *sorrow* and it can also mean *a deep and poignant distress caused by bereavement.*

Grief can relate to a loss, as in death, or a loss through the end of a relationship, such as divorce or one party moving away from the other. Grief can also relate to *your* moving away from a company or city or community with which you felt a strong sense of kinship.

Everyone deals with grief in his or her own way and the activity of moving through the inevitable sorrow and feelings of loss doesn't always follow a set time schedule.

Although everyone grieves in different ways, there are passages or parts to grief, some of which you may encounter and some you may not. Here are just a few:

DISBELIEF
Feelings of disbelief are at their highest immediately after the loss.

YEARNING
Missing a loved one (or whatever has been lost) may be the dominant grief response.

ANGER
Anger can take many forms and may take some time to reach its highest peak.

DEPRESSION
Feelings of extreme sadness may follow the anger and may last for weeks or months.

ACCEPTANCE

Although inevitable, acceptance may take many months or years. As time passes, acceptance of the loss grows as the other feelings are felt and released.

Some grief counselors advise that it takes a full year to fully grieve for a loved one. One has to go through a full calendar year of holidays, birthdays and anniversaries to experience the loss under these new circumstances, in order to fully grieve and let go. For some, it may take longer than a year, so be gentle with yourself.

Chances are, you've picked up this book (or perhaps someone gave you this book) in order to deal with your feelings of grief, heal those feelings and move on with your life. Although that may seem unlikely today, believe me when I tell you, you can and will heal from your loss. The purpose of this guidebook is to help you heal and begin to enjoy life again.

Relief for Today - Take good care of yourself

During this time, it is very important to take good care of yourself. Here are just a few things to keep in mind:

- Get your rest. Many people report that they need more sleep, both overnight and during the day to recover from a profound loss.

- Keep in mind good nutrition. Eat balanced meals and allow yourself a little indulgence from time to time. This is NOT a time for dieting, taking up a new eating plan or starving yourself. Eat what you would normally eat and take a multivitamin. Avoid abusing alcohol.

- Follow your medication regimen. If you are under a doctor's care and take daily prescription medications, please continue this regimen. It is especially important that you take all medications, as prescribed. SEE YOUR DOCTOR before making any changes to your medications, diet or exercise program.

- Use an energy clearing modality to help you release some of the stress you are feeling during this time. EFT (Emotional Freedom Technique) is a wonderful way to release pain, hurt and sadness. Also, journaling and meditation are great aids for clearing and releasing feelings and allowing you to heal and grow from this experience.

- Take a salt bath. Fill a tub with 1 cup Epsom salts and 1 cup baking soda. You may add 5 to 10 drops of any essential oil, such as lavender or chamomile. Or, use any good quality bath salts with essential oils. Make the water warm, but not too hot. Sit in it up to your neck for at least 20 minutes. This cleanses your aura, releases toxins from the body and relieves muscle cramps and pain. It is also very grounding and relaxing. You may also use pink Himalayan salt in the same way.

- See the information on Pg 14--22 on Essential Oils and Crystals for additional support. For starters, get some Lavender essential oil, which is easy to find and inexpensive. You can apply it to your wrists, inhale deeply 3 X and allow your feelings to surface and then release. Rose Quartz crystals are also easily obtained and inexpensive. Rose Quartz is a great crystal for heart healing and self-love.

- Stay with your exercise program. If you regularly run, walk or work out at a gym, continue this activity, as much as possible. If you can walk in your neighborhood, for example, rather than taking the time away from family to go to the gym, do this.

  Keep up your regular activities. SEE YOUR DOCTOR before you add an exercise program to your daily life.

- Lean on friends for support. If friends offer to help with meals or chores, allow them to do so. If you need to ask for help, in order to get through some of the plans you have to make, do this and know that the duties will go more smoothly with the help of a trusted friend. Sometimes, a friend can lend a shoulder to cry on or a friendly ear just to listen. Take advantage of such friends and family members in these instances.

- Go to a movie, a museum, a library or any activity that brings you joy. Please do not feel that you are dishonoring your loved one by enjoying yourself or participating in these activities.

- Get a massage, Reiki, reflexology, cranial sacral, BARS or other type of energy clearing or bodywork session. Not just once, but several times, as you are grieving, releasing and healing.

EFT –Basic Template

EFT (Emotional Freedom Technique) is an energy clearing technique that's based on traditional Chinese medicine and the ancient art of acupuncture. Instead of using needles, we tap right on the face and body, where an acupuncturist would put needles.

Acupuncturists say we have meridians or circuits in our body where electricity flows up or down these pathways. (All you have to do is walk across carpeting and reach out to touch someone and shock them to know this is true!)

And when you get a block in one of those lines of energy, then you've got symptoms or pain. What EFT does is break through the congestion. We tap and clear out the congestion or clear out the conflict, anything that's caught or trapped in our circuits. Then, we can relax and we have better circulation. Then, we can better handle emotional struggles. It's a stress relief technique or tool, and it gets to our core issues.

EFT was created initially as TFT (Thought Field Therapy) by Dr. Roger Callahan. It was very cumbersome and has various sequences of varying complexity, called algorithms, which are related to specific complaints. The theory goes that by tapping these points, a number of times, unwanted emotions can be released. A man named Gary Craig studied with Dr. Callahan and simplified the technique, teaching us to tap the same sequence of points, regardless of the situation or issue.

Although EFT has not been scientifically validated, it has been in use in America and around the world since 1995. Gary has made it his life's work to make EFT accessible to everyone. You can learn more at: **www.emofree.com**. At the official EFT website, you can view videos about how to use EFT and see documentation of its effectiveness for a myriad of physical, mental and emotional conditions. The most impressive work Gary has done with EFT involves its use at Veteran's Hospitals, helping vets deal with post traumatic stress disorder and a host of other emotional conditions.

Since I first wrote this book as a class in 2008, many other people have gotten involved in EFT. Sometimes, it is called Meridian Tapping, MTT (Meridian Tapping Technique), just "tapping" and many other names. There are more videos on YouTube now and the brother/sister team of Nick and Jessica Ortner have created The World Tapping Summit and written books about tapping. Their website is: **http://www.thetappingsolution.com/**

The main theory behind EFT is that all negative emotion is due to a disruption in the body's energy system. We are clearing or cleaning out the body's emotional system with EFT. Once you clear the energy system, the feelings become neutralized. This takes place when we tap on the energy system.

The feelings, in and of themselves, aren't bad. But most negative emotions come from some disturbance in our energy system. Unresolved feelings are major contributors to physical pain and disease. If you continue to have conflicts and emotional challenges, it breaks down your immune system. You get exhausted and when you over-do things and don't deal with problems in your life, your body can begin to break down. Stress is a major contributor to physical, emotional and mental conditions. With EFT, we treat the body, mind and spirit as a whole. You can release or relieve stress and allow your body to heal by tapping on the meridian points.

Recovering from the loss of someone we love is a difficult task and the missing part doesn't completely heal with EFT tapping. But EFT can help release the painful emotions that can inflict terrible pain and suffering. EFT can also help shorten the time it takes to recover, because you spend your time feeling and healing, rather than ignoring or stuffing your feelings into some dark, deep place.

Note: EFT was originally created with 8 Tapping Points. One was under the nipple and considered "too personal" for public classes and demonstrations, so Gary Craig deleted it. A lot of the tapping scripts you see online feature only 7 or 8 Tapping Points.

I studied with EFT Master Lindsay Kenny, who uses 10 tapping points. With 10 tapping points (she added the Top of the Head and Wrist points) you can move energy from 14 meridians of the body. I use Lindsay Kenny's tapping points and chart, having paid a fee for the rights to use the chart.

Basic EFT Tapping Script

In order to utilize EFT, you need to understand a simple technique for tapping. The most simple way is to follow along with someone, while you look at a Tapping Chart. So, read on and tap along as I explain the easy steps.

EFT Tapping Points—10 Main Points

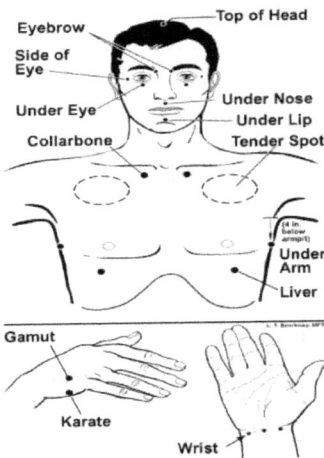

Eyebrow
Side of Eye
Under Eye
Collarbone

Top of Head
Under Nose
Under Lip
Tender Spot

(4 in. below armpit)
Under Arm
Liver

Gamut
Karate
Wrist

1-Top of head
2-Eyebrow
3-Side of Eye
4-Under Eye
5-Under Nose
6-Chin
7-Collarbone
8-Under Arm (4" from armpit)
9-Rib (Liver)
10-Wrist

Set-Up—Use Sore Spot
          Or Karate Chop
                    Point
The Gamut Point is used
    in situations where we
    may have hit a plateau
    and we want to move on.
    Just rub or tap the spot.
These Tapping Points clear energy
from 14 meridians!

Graphic Used with Permission © 2009 Lindsay Kenny

1. Focus in on how you feel. Let's take the example of "I feel sad." How intense is your feeling? 10 = VERY INTENSE and 1 = Not Very   (Put the number here) _____

2. Look at the Tapping Chart above. Tap the Karate Chop Point on your <u>Non-Dominant Hand</u> with 3-4 fingers of your <u>Dominant Hand</u> (the hand you write with) and Say the **Set Up Sentence** 3 X: (Use your own words... these are examples only.)

   Even though I feel sad about losing my loved one, I deeply and completely love and accept myself.

3. Create a **Reminder Phrase** from the sentence above. For example, say the phrase "I feel sad" <u>and</u> Tap 5 to 7 times on each of the 10 points shown. Use 2-3 fingers of the <u>Dominant Hand</u> to Tap on each of the points shown.

•	Top of Head	I feel sad
•	Side of Eyebrow	I feel sad
•	Side of Eye	I feel sad
•	Under Eye	I feel sad
•	Under Nose	I feel sad
•	Under Lip	I feel sad
•	Collarbone	I feel sad
•	Under Armpit	I feel sad
•	Under Rib	I feel sad
•	Wrist	I feel sad

4. Assess how you feel. What is the number now? Is it lower? If not, do another round. You want to reduce the number to 1 or 2. You may feel a shift, a change in your energy. You may sigh, shiver, yawn or just feel lighter. Each of these is a signal that you are clearing energy. Welcome each sign with gratitude. Say "Thank you" for the healing. It is a baby step toward feeling better! So, seal your healing with gratitude!

5. Have a glass of water nearby and take a drink or two. Staying hydrated is a great way to continue the healing, without taxing your body or energy system.

Of course, a feeling such as "I'm sad," is very general in nature. While you are tapping, you may have other ideas that come to mind. When you are finished with the round, write down any other feelings you experienced and complete a round of EFT on each feeling.

Now that you have an idea of how EFT works, you can use a more specific script for tapping, one that will help move even more blocks out of the way and release sadness and stress from your life. Please note that each of these scripts are only examples of wording. In order to get the most benefit from EFT, you will want to change the words to your own words and be sure to use inflection in your voice. You will remove more blocks with inflection and feeling, rather than simply reading the scripts in a monotone voice. Yes, your intention is key in this work. When you set your intention to clear blocks and make the way for peace in your life, you will achieve much more.

Here's another script for grief that will help you voice your own feelings.

EFT for Feelings of Grief or Sadness

Focus on your feeling of grief or sadness around the loss of your loved one, friend or relationship. Allow yourself to really feel this. Rate it now _____ (10 = intense) ("*Sad about my loss*" is used below – use your own words)

What other feelings describe your grief or sadness? Write those here, even if they don't make sense or seem silly. Write a different word or short phrase on each line:

1._____
2._____
3. _____
4. _____
5. _____
6. _____
7. _____
8._____
9._____
10._____

1. Tap the Karate Chop Point with your <u>Dominant Hand</u> and Say the Set Up Sentence 3 X. (The one shown here is an example. Use your own words.)

   • Even though I feel sad about my loss, I deeply and completely love and accept myself.

2. Now, Tap each of the 10 tapping points as you say one of the phrases that you wrote in the 10 spaces up above for each tapping point.

   Top of head: Phrase on line #1
   Eyebrow: Phrase on line #2
   Side of Eye: Phrase on line #3 . . . and so on . .
   Under Eye:
   Under Nose:
   Chin:

Collarbone:
Under Arm:
Under Rib:
Wrist:

3. Now, how do you feel?_____

   How has the feeling changed?_____

   How would you describe it?

   _____

   On a scale of 1 to 10, what is the number now?

   The goal is to reduce the number to 1 or 2. Since so many of us are such perfectionists, we don't aim for "0" as that might prove frustrating! Restate your overall feeling now, and do another round of EFT.

4. For example, Tap the Karate Chop Point and Say 3 X "Even though I **feel depressed**, I deeply and completely love and accept myself." **OR** "Even though I **still** feel sad, I deeply and completely love and accept myself."

5. Tap the 10 points with new feeling or "I still feel sad" or a combination of these phrases.

6. Assess how you feel. What is the number now?

7. Say "Thank You" and seal your healing with gratitude.

8. Have a drink of water. You need lots of water as you clear old feelings.

You can also use this for other feelings, such as fear, sense of betrayal, anger, envy, etc. Recognize that you may feel other feelings toward the person you lost (whether through death, loss of the relationship, the person moving away, etc.) Also, know that no feeling, in and of itself, is bad or wrong; it's just a feeling. The power of EFT lies in your "owning" your feelings and allowing yourself to feel what you feel. There is something very liberating about just allowing yourself to feel sad or angry or whatever you feel. It is an incredible type of stress relief to tap until the emotional charge around the feeling is gone or greatly reduced.

At this point in coaching sessions, I am usually asked, "What if I start crying and I can't stop?" Or, "What if I get bogged down and can't even get out of my house?"

Just go ahead and cry. And TAP! The best example I have ever heard about this is the analogy of a John Wayne movie where he has to jump on the stage coach to take the reins of some runaway horses. Does he try to pull up the reins, maybe breaking them, or falling off and being of no help to the damsel inside the stage coach? No, he allows the horses to run. And, sooner, rather than later, the horses tire out and stop. Then, he takes charge of the reins and brings the stage coach back to where it needs to go.

This is also true of you and your emotions. When we really sit with our grief, sadness or anger, it is amazing how short the time frame of that intense emotion really is. It is usually our fear of what "might" happen that causes us to keep these emotions pushed down inside. When we really feel what we feel, especially when tapping along with the feeling, it is a quick process to clear the block and return to peace and calm.

Essential Oils to Support You

I have been using essential oils for several years, beginning with the use of Rosemary and Peppermint in my shower gel. I went to a spa a number of years ago and it had Aveda shower gel with rosemary and mint. I loved it so much that I bought a bottle. It was $17 for a small bottle. Yikes!

When that was gone, I went to Whole Foods and bought a small bottle of Rosemary essential oil and Peppermint essential oil. I got a bottle of Dove body wash and added a few drops of the oils. Wonderful! I've been doing it ever since.

Now, this was purely intuitive on my part. Something in me resonated with the Rosemary and the Mint in the Aveda product. I've continued to use it for well over 10 years now.

Want to know what Rosemary does? Rosemary is the Oil of Transition! Amazing. It also The Oil of Knowledge and addresses confusion and difficulty in adjusting, transitioning and gaining better a perspective.

What an incredible oil to add to my life, way back when I was creating my practice in Hypnosis, studying mediumship and becoming the person I was meant to be!

And Peppermint? It is the Oil of a Buoyant Heart and helps in letting go of pessimism and heaviness. Helps in letting go of pain and gives you the strength to face your emotional reality. WOW! And, it invigorates me! What a great way to start my day!

I use this DAILY in my shower, as the last thing I do. I put some in my hands, inhale three times and then lather it on my heart area, arms and legs. I breathe in the aroma and allow it to go deeply into my cells. Then I say my prayer for the day.

Why do I continue to use essential oils in my life? Well, did you know that people have been using essential oils since time began? Essential oils are made from live plants and flowers, by distillation, cold pressing or resin tapping. When you buy a certified pure therapeutic grade essential oil by a company such as doTERRA®, Young Living or Aura Cacia, you are getting the lifeblood of the plant and a natural way to take your body back to its state of wellbeing.

Each essential oil's scent activates the limbic system, which is the brain's center of emotion and memory. In fact, when you inhale an essential oil, it travels through your nasal cavity and directly into the brain in a matter of seconds. Each of the essential oils has therapeutic properties, such as calming, balancing, releasing, etc., and the aroma molecules send messages to the brain. So, if you inhale an essential oil that has a calming effect on the body, then the brain receives a message to relax. Similarly, when you apply essential oils topically to the body, the molecules enter all of the cells of the body within a matter of about 20 minutes. It is important to know that even when the oils are applied to the body, the aroma also goes into the brain, by way of the olfactory system.

I recommend that you use a good quality essential oil such as doTERRA®, Young Living or Aura Cacia. My personal favorite is doTERRA® and most of the oils and oil blends mentioned in this book are doTERRA® brand essential oils. There is a difference between a good quality essential oil, such as doTERRA® and an off-brand from a discount store. Make sure the essential oils you buy are Certified Pure Therapeutic Grade essential oils.

Here are some other ways to use Essential Oils:

1. Find an oil that resonates for you and apply on inside of wrists. (pulse points) Inhale 3 X and then go about your day. Just a drop on each wrist will do. I make Rollerballs of the oils I like the most and this makes it easy to apply.
2. Put a drop or two on a tissue or cotton ball and inhale 3 X.
3. Short on time? Just open a bottle of essential oils, hold under your nose and inhale 3X.
4. Put a 2 to 3 drops in a diffuser with water and turn on to diffuse in your space. You can even add crystals to your diffuser, also!
5. Put 2 or 3 drops in a glass bottle with ½ c alcohol and ½ c distilled water. Stick in some reeds, bamboo sticks/skewers and allow the scent to fill the room.
6. Use essential oils to help you sleep. Make a roller ball of 20 drops Lavender and 7 drops Vetiver and put on your feet before bedtime. This works great for kids, too!
7. You can also put Lavender in your diffuser for sleepy time. Great for kids!
8. Put your favorite essential oil around your belly button for an uplifting and healing break in your day. Around, NOT IN your belly button!
9. Use Frankincense or Lavender on your temples for a headache. (Check by smelling first. Frankincense is really strong to me and doesn't work for me like Lavender does.)
10. Use Frankincense or your favorite oil in the diffuser or on pulse points for meditation.

11. Rub your favorite oil on your chest, shoulders and the back of the neck. This helps to seal and protect your etheric field. (Try Citrus Bliss Blend by doTERRA®)

12. Look at a Reflexology chart for the FEET and put oils on the places that represent certain organs for healing.

13. You can also put oil on your body where the organ is located for healing. Here are some examples:
Kidneys – Fear
Spleen/Stomach – Worry
Lungs – Sadness
Liver/Gall Bladder – Anger
Heart - Joy

14. One of my favorite Rollerball recipes is Liquid Xanax. It is 20 drops of doTERRA® Balance Blend and 20 drops of doTERRA® Serenity Blend and fill up with coconut oil in a rollerball. I use this for deep healing of Inner Child issues, family stuff and any personal stuff that comes up during the day. You can get Rollerballs at Whole Foods and on Amazon. They are empty GLASS Bottles that hold 1/3 of an ounce of liquid. You can buy kits of 12 or more and each one comes with a Rollerball stopper and a lid.

15. Forgive Blend by doTERRA® is great when we are working through forgiving, releasing and moving on. Put in a Rollerball, so you can use throughout your day. For a single oil or oil blend, I recommend 20 drops per Rollerball for adults. You will want to use less drops of the essential oil for children.

16. For Grief, you can use the Liquid Xanax, which will support you gently, while you grieve. There

are also these oils that you can use in a rollerball or diffuser, which help you with the different passages of Grief:

Shock: Lavender, Neroli

Sadness: Joyful Blend by doTERRA®, Breathe Blend by doTERRA® or Frankincense

Anger: Calming Blend by doTERRA® or Roman Chamomile

Fear: Bergamot, Grapefruit

Releasing: Bergamot, Roman Chamomile or Sandalwood

Acceptance and Moving On: Coriander, Wild Orange and Frankincense, Ylang Ylang, Peppermint

Feeling Locked in Grief: Balance Blend by doTERRA®, Myrrh or Lemon

17. Rub a Rollerball of your favorite oil on your palm and hold gently over the nose of a crying or upset child/baby. Watch them relax, as they breathe in. Remember to look up age appropriate use for some oils, such as eucalyptus or melaleuca. Lavender is a safe one to use in this instance.

18. Apply a drop on index finger and apply behind ear. Duplicate on the other ear. (Be careful putting on fingers. Wash carefully with SOAP and water or wipe off with coconut oil. You don't want to get oils in your eyes. If you do, flush with oil, not water!!)

Essential Oils — aka concentrated liquid magic, gifted to us on behalf of the Plant and Flower People — aid in activating life-affirming vibrational and emotional states of health and well-being. **-Stacey Robyn**

Crystals to Support You

All of the years that I was buying crystals and making jewelry for myself and others, I was intuitively using crystals for emotional support and healing. Now that I have more knowledge and training, I can do this in a more conscious fashion, although I still rely on my intuition to guide me in some instances.

In August of 2015, I lost my last living Uncle. He was my Mom's older brother and was truly the patriarch of our family, after their parents passed away in the early '70's. He lived to be 93.

To prepare for attending the funeral, I grabbed my Rollerball of Liquid Xanax and called my crystal teacher, Michelle Welch of **www.soultopia.guru** for support. She suggested that I get an Archangel Azrael bracelet of yellow calcite. Yellow calcite is the perfect stone for sadness and grief. She has these available at SoulTopia, so I drove over on my lunch hour, two days before the funeral. While I was there, she also helped me select crystals from the Crystal Bar for grief: Apache Tear, Honey Calcite, Rose Quartz, Amethyst and Smokey Quartz. She put them in a little silk bag and gave me a card with the recipe on it for reference.

So, on the day of the funeral, I applied Liquid Xanax to each of my wrists, put on two Archangel Azrael bracelets and tucked the Liquid Xanax and the silk bag of crystals in my purse. I also put a piece of Carnelian in each of my pockets. Carnelian is great for the Sacral Chakra and shores up motivation, endurance, leadership and courage.

I reapplied the Liquid Xanax several times that day. I laughed and cried. I talked with my Mom, my siblings, my cousins. I flew home and shared with my husband:

"I felt supported. I felt that with the essential oils and crystals, I was held in the arms of my angels and was free to feel my feelings, without the fear of being overwhelmed."

So how do crystals "work"? You may know that everything vibrates, including humans. And, as humans, our frequency varies with our moods, health and other factors. Crystals, on the other hand each have a set oscillating rate, due to their internal, molecular structure. Each crystal has a specific geometric pattern, which repeats and never changes.

"Because of their special geometric patterning, crystals are able to tap into universal energy patterns and frequencies that science is only beginning to discover."
-Dr. Richard Gerber

"We're so easily energetically-influenced, partly due to our emotions & partly due to our mainly non-crystalline structure. Unlike crystals, our body's vibrations can move out of its dominant oscillatory rate (DOR) so very easily when we experience ANY TYPE OF STRESS.
We're also made of many varying oscillatory rates as our organs & even cells have all their own DORs."
-Hibiscus Moon

For example, Clear Quartz has what is called a "trigonal" geometric pattern. Always. And, its dominant oscillatory rate (or frequency) never varies. This is true of all crystals.

Since humans entropy, or decline over time and vary in our frequency, we can easily "entrain" or be influenced by crystals. Since it is easier for two systems to work in cooperation than opposition, by spending time with crystals, we can raise our personal vibration.

So, when you feel low or "off" you can wear or just be in the presence of crystals to adjust your personal frequency. This is especially important with emotional issues, such as grief and sadness. As I stated earlier, I feel that crystals work to support us as we grieve. The crystals join with our angels to hold us in loving arms, so we are safe and free to feel what we feel, and to release those feelings when we are ready and move on.

What are some other crystals to use for emotional support and healing? Well, you can always Google "crystals for _____" and get lots of information. There are also many wonderful crystal guides and books available. I recommend those by Katrina Raphaell, Adrienne Goff, Philip Permutt and Judy Hall. Go to Half Price Books and let a book "pick" you.

Here is a list of crystals from Michelle Welch of SoulTopia Academy to get you started:

Yellow Calcite	Sadness
Apache Tear	Grief
Tiger Iron	Harmony
Red Calcite	Energy and Willpower
Lepidolite	Stress & Anxiety
Onyx (Blue)	Self Control
Fluorite	Focus
Sodalite	Speaking your truth
Malachite	Safe Travel
Amethyst	Homesickness
Apatite	Metabolism
Shungite	Cleanse and Protect

To recap, here is the "crystal recipe" Michelle created for me for supporting me through my recent loss:

Rose Quartz   Apache Tear   Honey Calcite
Smokey Quartz   Amethyst

I carried these stones in the silk bag in my purse for weeks and even slept with them under my pillow for a few days before and after my uncle's memorial service.

Special Note: I'd also like to point out that Clear Quartz will amplify or enhance the healing power of any crystal. Think about computer chips, watches and other electronic devices. Yes, clear quartz crystals power these modern machines. Get some clear quartz "points" or small clear quartz pieces to keep on hand. Clear Quartz Crystals can be among the least expensive and hardest working crystals in your toolkit.

How to incorporate crystals into your daily life:

-Buy as jewelry or get beads and make into jewelry
-Put in small bags and carry in purse, briefcase or backpack
-Put under your pillow or on your nightstand
-Carry small, smooth stones in your pocket
-Display crystals in your home, yard, office or workplace
-Add crystals to key chains or lanyards
-Add crystals to your bath
-Make a grid of crystals for a specific purpose
-Make gem elixers with crystals and add to teas, bath salts, water, etc.

Here's another recipe from Michelle Welch that helps you to call in your angels for healing:
Angelite   Selenite   Blue Kyanite.

I have a small bag of these crystals that I keep at my office!

Learn more about Michelle and her SoulTopia Crystal Healing Academy at: **www.soultopia.guru**

Prayer & Meditation

Especially in times of grief and sadness, you may feel that you are all alone. You may also feel that you can't seem to connect to God or Divine Source or Spirit. (Insert your favorite word or phrase for your personal Deity here) You may feel that something is wrong, even wrong with you in this instance. Prayer is a way to request help for yourself, often on the spot and without reservation! Many people "forget" to pray or feel that God won't "hear" their prayer. But, prayer is a great way to quiet the mind and call on supernatural powers to help strengthen us in times of need.

When we pray, when we ask for help, we are met halfway by the Great All That Is. Did you know that when we close our eyes, our brain immediately goes into Alpha brain waves, the brain waves of meditation? Just the act of closing the eyes and bowing the head, prepares the way for the mind and body to claim the power of prayer. So adopt this prayerful pose and feel yourself being lifted up to a beautiful connection with God and the Angels. It's as if the entire Universe hears your plea for healing and guidance. Some believe that you create a "sacred space" which is filled with your energy, and you can return to this place, again and again to ask for help or find a shoulder to cry on.

The following is a prayer I use often:

"Mother, Father God, Creator of all that is, I ask that you wrap your arms of love around me. Please bring me to that special place where I can find peace, love and guidance. Let your love and wisdom flow through me today. I am hurting and I ask you to take my pain and transform it, so that I can feel safe and calm."

I now visualize or imagine a white light from the Highest Source entering through the top of my head and totally filling me with this Divine light. Then, I take a deep breath to relax and then allow myself to feel a connection to Divine Source.

Your prayer can be simple, like this one, or you can pray the Lord's Prayer or any prayer that comforts you. You may have your own special prayer from childhood, such as praying the rosary, so pray it. You might be comforted by singing a favorite hymn. This can be like a prayer, as well. Singing "Amazing Grace" or "Jesus Loves Me" comforts me when I am sad.

Meditation

Now, you may be thinking, I'm just getting a handle on my emotions and now, you want me to *meditate*?

Meditation may be more (or less!) than what you think it is. Meditation is a great way to go within and just "be." And "being" may be a lot more important right now than "doing" for you.

There are a number of ways to meditate:
- Guided meditation with an App, Mp3 or on-line audio.

- Breathing meditation, where you follow your breath and just sit quietly.

- Walking meditation, where you walk and still your mind. This can be indoors or out in nature, like a park or a labyrinth at a church or spiritual center. You can also walk in a public place, like a shopping mall, where you wear ear buds with music or a guided meditation. Some people like the activity of walking.

- Knitting, sewing or handwork of any kind can also be used as a meditation. Any activity short of reading, watching TV or communicating with another can be used in this way.

- There are also several new styles of meditation audios that use "brain wave therapy" to help you achieve meditation states easier and faster. You can find these on the internet or Amazon. One I recommend comes from Kelly Howell and requires the use of stereo headphones. Here's a recap from her website:

  For over two decades, Brain Sync has been the leading developer of brain wave therapy programs. Now you can consistently enter into peak experience brain states and reap powerful benefits of brain wave entrainment therapy. **www.brainsync.com**

Brain Sync works by combining music with "binaural beats" and may include voice commands, which are shared in Kelly Howell's soft, yet powerful voice. I use one of Kelly's audios almost every day. Her new app for iPhone is called MeditateMe and comes with 3 different meditations, each in 3 different lengths: 10, 20 or 20 minutes.

When you are first starting out, I recommend no more than 5 or 10 minutes. Gradually, you can build up to 20 or 30 minutes.

There is nothing "wrong" with using guided meditations. I find that guided meditations are best for beginners, especially those of us with "monkey mind" or ADD. Some days I use the guided track and some days I use the music and beats only. Now that I have experience meditating, I can close my eyes and go within and find my personal sanctuary just about anywhere. This helps me take a break in my day and can also help me obtain guidance when necessary.

Journaling & Gratitude

The process of journaling can really help you put words to your feelings and process a lot of feelings that may have been held in your heart and mind for a long time.

How to journal? It's easy . . . just get a spiral notebook, a yellow pad or any type of notebook that has sheets of paper. Or, you can create a journal on your computer by opening a Word document and adding to the file each time you write.

After you decide whether you are going to write or type, just put the date at the top of the page and begin writing. Some days, you may just put the things you did that day. Sometimes, you may put feelings, such as:

"Today, I'm sad about _____. And it makes me even more sad that nobody cares about how I feel."

You can also put goals, dreams, ambitions, desires of the heart...you get the idea. Make it your own!

Remember, this is yours and you get to write whatever you want. No one will see it and no one is going to edit it or judge it. It is ESPECIALLY important that you do not edit or judge or critique what you write. Just let it flow. Some days you may write a few paragraphs, and on other days, you may write two or three pages. Don't make demands. Again, just let it flow.

The important thing is to capture how you feel and let it out. A wonderful thing about journaling is how it helps you track your progress. In about six months, you can look back at your journal and see how far you've come.

For your grieving process, I recommend that you write every day. If you miss a day, don't beat yourself up...just write the next day. After you see the benefits, you'll get into a regular rhythm.

Gratitude

Why gratitude? Well, when we can find anything in our life to appreciate, we reconnect with our Creator and this sustains us on our earthly journey. Find some time today to give thanks and see how it brings a smile to your lips. What might you find to be grateful for?

- Being alive

- A wonderful cup of coffee

- A smile from a friend

- A hug from a child

- Friends to help around your recent loss

- A beautiful sunset

Put three things for which you are grateful in your journal today and see what a difference it makes in your life. Or, silently name three things before you fall asleep tonight.

To learn more about gratitude, visit a wonderful website: **www.gogratitude.com**, which celebrates gratitude and where more than 1 million folks have chimed in to share stories. You can also pick up any one of a number of gratitude journals in a bookstore or on Amazon.com

One of my favorite master teachers is Esther Hicks of Abraham-Hicks and she has this to say about "appreciation", which is a close cousin to gratitude:

"The Rampage of Appreciation Game can be played anywhere and at any time because it is easily played simply by directing pleasant thoughts in your mind. Write your thoughts on paper to enhance the process, but it is not necessary.

Begin by looking around your immediate environment and gently noticing something that pleases you. Try to hold your attention on this pleasing object as you consider how wonderful, beautiful, or useful it is. And as you focus upon it longer, your positive feelings about it will increase.

Now, notice your improved feeling, and be appreciative of the way you feel. Then, once your good feeling is noticeably stronger than when you began, look around your environment and choose another pleasing object for your positive attention.

Make it your objective to choose objects of attention that easily evoke your appreciation, for this is not a process of finding something troubling and fixing it; this is a process of practicing the higher vibrations. The longer you focus upon things that feel good to you, the easier it is for you to maintain those vibrational frequencies that feel good."

Source: http://www.abraham-hicks.com/

Can't find anything to appreciate right now? Use this EFT script and create your own Rampage of Appreciation.

EFT for GRATITUDE

If you want more in your life to be grateful for, focus on the appreciation you already feel for what and who you have in your life. Start by addressing the genuine mood or feeling state you feel right now, then move into appreciation and gratitude.

Tap on Karate Chop Point:
Even though I feel a little down right now, I choose to focus on positive emotions...
Even though I don't feel very positive right now, I accept who I am and how I feel...
Even though I'm wallowing in self-pity right now, I accept all of me and how I feel.

EYEBROW: *I'm always afraid of what might happen*
SIDE OF EYE: *What if something bad happens to me?*
UNDER EYE: *I feel the fear in my vibration every day*
UNDER NOSE: *I can feel the fear no matter what I do*
CHIN: *I don't feel safe unless I'm feeling worried*
COLLARBONE: *I'm afraid to let go of my fear*
UNDER ARM: *I don't know how to feel any other way*
HEAD: *What if I can't let go of my fear?*

EYEBROW: *I keep focusing on the negative.*
SIDE OF EYE: *Maybe I don't want to be positive.*
UNDER EYE: *I feel frustrated about so many things.*
UNDER NOSE: *It's hard to change my focus.*
CHIN: *I keep focusing on the negative.*
COLLARBONE: *I feel so overwhelmed.*
UNDER ARM: *It's hard to change my focus.*
HEAD: *I don't know if I want to be grateful...*

After you have used **EFT** to relieve the focus on the negative, move towards more positive and appreciative thoughts and statements:

EYEBROW: *I have decided to notice what I appreciate.*
SIDE OF EYE: *I'm ready to change my focus right now.*
UNDER EYE: *I appreciate how much I feel grateful for in my life.*
UNDER NOSE: *I choose to notice the many blessings in my life.*
CHIN: *I appreciate who I am and the miracles in my life.*
COLLARBONE: *I have so much abundance right now, and I look forward to more.*
UNDER ARM: *I appreciate all the abundance flowing into my life.*
HEAD: *I appreciate who I am and how I feel.*
EYEBROW: *I love feeling grateful*
SIDE OF EYE: *I choose to feel good no matter what*
UNDER EYE: *I feel appreciation for being alive*
UNDER NOSE: *I love who I am and how I feel*
CHIN: *I'm grateful for my life*
COLLARBONE: *I appreciate so much in my life*
UNDER ARM: *I'm grateful for the clarity in my life*

Take a deep breath and then continue Tapping:

HEAD: *I love feeling so joyful*
EYEBROW: *I love feeling good*
SIDE OF EYE: *I appreciate feeling so grateful*
UNDER EYE: *I appreciate who I am*
UNDER NOSE: *I love who I am becoming*
CHIN: *I'm grateful for all my feelings*
COLLARBONE: *I appreciate the guidance I am getting*
UNDER ARM: *I'm grateful for who I am*
HEAD: *I love feeling such joy*

After this marathon of gratitude tapping, measure how you feel afterwards. You can then tap on any new issues that pop up. These are the "yes, but . . ." feelings.

Two other ideas from Carol Look:

The *Gratitude List* involves writing down on paper, once a day, all that you feel grateful for. Write it out any time of day that feels right to you. If you write your list at night, it may keep you up because some folks have a hard time settling down afterwards. ☺

The *Gratitude Walk* is the act of reciting your gratitude list out loud, while you are walking outside in nature, swinging your arms, breathing deeply and thanking the Universe for all the blessings in your life. Both of these methods are thrilling. And don't forget to express your appreciation directly to others. Doing so changes lives!

Source: Carol Look © 2006 Attracting Abundance
Newsletter #33 Used with permission.

*"The moment you accept what troubles you've
been given, the door will open."*

-Rumi

Section Two – Symptoms of Grief

Everyone grieves differently and the symptoms of grief can show up in many ways:

- **Shock and disbelief**
- **Sadness, including intense sorrow and pain**
- **Guilt**
- **Bitterness**
- **Anger**
- **Fear**
- **Lack of trust**
- **Physical symptoms**

Because everyone experiences and recovers from death or loss in her or his own way, you may not experience all of the symptoms shown. I'm going to share a few tools and energy clearing techniques for each of the symptoms. My prayer is that you may connect with one or two of the tools and you are able to experience relief and healing.

Shock and Disbelief: I can't believe my loved one is gone!

You may initially find it hard to believe that your loved one is really gone. You may hope that when you wake up tomorrow, you will find that this has been a very bad dream and that when you walk around the corner, your loved one is there, waiting for you.

By being open to these feelings of disbelief and working through them, you can begin to balance yourself and make it through the first few days and weeks after a loss.
You may now be familiar with EFT and you may have used it a time or two. The EFT script shown below can be used to "talk out" your feelings and is only a sample to

get you started. Read the script and use inflection in your voice to really FEEL what you are feeling. Then, when the script ends, continue to "talk and tap" and allow yourself to say whatever comes to mind.

Special Note: The words shown below are shown for example, only. If different words resonate for you, please use your own words. You may say "this grief" or "this loss" or "I feel lost" or anything that <u>feels</u> right for you.

Before you begin, focus in on how you feel. With the example of "I am so sad," how intense is your feeling? 10 = VERY INTENSE and 1 = Not Very _____

EFT – Talk and Tap

Say the Sentence shown and Tap the Karate Chop point:

Karate Chop: Even though I am so sad, sadness consumes my thoughts and my sadness is so big that I don't know if I will ever recover, I deeply and completely love and accept myself.

Karate Chop: Even though this sadness is so deep, this sadness about _____'s death, this sadness can't be described and I feel this sadness is never going to go away, I deeply and completely love and accept myself.

Karate Chop: Even though I feel this way, I deeply and completely love and accept myself and I honor my journey as I sit here today.

Tap the Tapping Point shown and say this phrase or something similar that resonates for you

Top of Head: The feeling of my sadness around _____'s
passing

Eyebrow: This sadness that threatens to consume me
Side of Eye: Sadness
Under Eye: *I AM SO SAD I CAN'T BREATHE*
Under nose: Sadness
Chin: This sadness, it means I really loved _____.
Collarbone: How can I live without _____in my life?
Underarm: _____ was very important to me
Ribs: Nothing was more important (or similar feelings)
Wrist: I loved _____very much

Take a deep breath and continue tapping

Top of Head: My feeling of sadness stops me from loving anyone else (revise if necessary)
Eyebrow: This sadness keeps me from my work
Side of Eye: My sadness
Under Eye: *MY SADNESS* keeps me from my children and family (revise as necessary)
Under nose: I can't stop being so sad
Chin: This sadness is all around me
Collarbone: How can I get through this?
Underarm: Sadness is my friend
Ribs: My sadness is here and _____ is not
Wrist: I loved _____very much.

Assess how you feel now. What is the number now? ___

You can always do another round with "I still feel some of this (sadness)." OR you can really "talk and tap," by just tapping on each of the ten tapping points, while you talk out loud about how you are feeling. Sometimes, this is the best kind of healing. Just owning how you feel and allowing the feelings to just "be".

When you are finished tapping, say "Thank You" and seal your healing with gratitude. Take a drink of water to rehydrate yourself. Remember that a yawn, shiver or just feeling lighter means that you have cleared something from your energy system.

Crystals and Essential Oils to Support You

When you are initially dealing with the loss of a loved one or friend, Lavender essential oils may support the feelings of disbelief and shock. You can make a rollerball and apply to wrists, inhaling 3X after each application. Feel free to apply several times during your day and again before you go to sleep. In fact, Lavender is an excellent essential oil for sleep and you may want to apply to the soles of your feet and undersides of your toes.

Crystals to help you during this time include Chrysoprase, Yellow Calcite, Pyrite, Rutilated Quartz and Rose Quartz. The Rutilated Quartz helps repair the damage done by any type of trauma and the Rose Quartz heals the Heart Chakra. Remember to add Clear Quartz points to amplify the results of any crystal you choose to utilize for this part of your journey. I find it very comforting to put your crystals in a small, drawstring bag and place it under your pillow at night.

Sadness, Including Intense Sorrow and Pain

Whether it's a few days or weeks (or months) after the day of your initial loss, you will cross the threshold of **shock and disbelief** and move into **sadness** or mourning for your loved one. During these times, the friends who comforted you at first with meals and phone calls may have fallen away. There may be a greater sense of feeling alone and truly missing the loved one who has passed on. The following tools may help you during this time.

The following meditation is a wonderful way to connect with the profound sense of loss that may seem overwhelming at times. You may read along with the italicized portion below.

Sat Yam Meditation for Grief, Anger or Depression

By Laura Bruno – from a Blog dated Nov 5, 2008 (Based on a meditation by Yogiraj Alan Finger. Used with permission. The italics used below are mine (PJ Spur) to help you see the actual meditation instructions easily.)

When grief or loss overwhelms us, we instinctively choose fight or flight–both forms of denial. According to Elizabeth Kubler-Ross, denial marks the first stage of a five-part process, followed by anger, bargaining, depression and acceptance. If all recovery requires a progression through at least two of these stages, then how can we move through them faster? So many of my coaching clients remain stuck because of current reactions to very old grief. They don't want to dissect their experiences; they want to move past them. Now.

A meditation using the syllables "sat yam" (rhymes with "but" and "yawn") offers a powerful way to do just that. I first discovered this ancient technique on Yogi Raj Alan Finger's wonderful CD, "Life Enhancing Meditations," in which he leads listeners through a seated process. I found it effective in moving through my own emotions and began to share the method with clients whose reactions to grief continued to get the better of them. To my delight, they started practicing the meditation for a few minutes each day, and their anger and attachments began to fade. I've recommended it so many times over the years–and with such good results–that I decided to share the meditation here.

If you think of the old saying, "When life gives you lemons, make lemonade," this meditation gives you another option. It functions like a garbage disposal for old emotions that no longer serve us. What happens when we throw lemons in a garbage disposal? All that old, nasty smelling junk that sits in the sink and makes it stink, suddenly smells fresh. The lemon completely disappears, leaving only a fresh, invigorating scent and free-flowing water.

To begin the process, get as comfortable as you can without falling asleep. (Yogiraj Alan Finger recommends sitting upright; however, I encourage clients to use this meditation in the moment, whenever a new betrayal, loss or irritation threatens to turn into lasting grief or anger.) So, get as comfortable as you can and preferably close your eyes. Gradually bring yourself into your heart. If you can't get out of your head, imagine a ladder descending from your brain to your heart, and step down each rung with each breath, until you can step into your heart center.

Once in your heart, concentrate on your breath, imagining it flowing directly in and out of your heart center (at the center of your chest, not actually your physical heart!). Breathe like this for a minute or so.

On your next inhalation, inhale through your heart center and imagine you're dragging all your old grief, anger, loss, betrayal and attachments in with the breath. If you have a lot of emotions, you might imagine them wrapped in cloth that you drag in with the breath. You might also think of them as barnacles attaches to silk. Use whatever image comes to mind most easily. Inhale deeply, dragging all this old junk up to the crown (top) of your head, silently saying to yourself, "sat" (rhymes with "but").

Once you reach the end of your inhale at the crown of your head, exhale through your crown and imagine all that old stuff releasing out the top of your head. As you exhale, silently say to yourself, the sound, "yam" (rhymes with "hum"), imagining the sound carrying away all your grief and emotions. (I like to imagine huge wings opening up to the sound "yam" and taking flight with all the things I no longer need.)

Return to your heart and repeat: inhale, dragging all the remaining emotions into your heart with the sound "sat," dragging all that stuff up to your crown, and then releasing through the top of your head with an exhalation and the sound "yam." Inhale, release, repeat.

(You need not worry about "polluting" the world with all these "negative" emotions, because when something releases through your crown, it undergoes a spiritual transmutation and simply becomes uncharged energy.)

Continue to repeat the sat yam inhalation/exhalation process until you feel light in your heart and have difficulty finding enough "stuff" to drag in with your inhale. Once you've reached a good stopping point, enjoy this lighter, cleaner space of your heart and know that you can return here any time by inviting the grief into your heart, transforming it through breath and sound, and releasing it through the crown of the head.

This meditation works, in part, because it reconnects the head and the heart, reversing traditional sounds associated with their chakras. "Sat," meaning "truth" or "true identity," usually corresponds to the seventh chakra, while "yam" represents the sound of the fourth (or heart) chakra. By reversing these sounds, this meditation encourages consciousness in the heart and a connection between "hridaya" (gateway to the highest level of reality) and our point of union with the Divine. Head and heart become an integrated whole.

Because this meditation involves a bit of multi-tasking (concurrent breath, sound, visualization), people often wonder if they can practice isolated parts of it. "Can't I just breathe deeply? What if I forget the sounds?" My own and others' experiences find the whole greater than the sum of its parts in this case. Deep breathing will help anyone deal with stress, but without the mantra and visuals, deep breathing does not act as a grief eater. Deep breaths will relax you, but they will not cause "lemons" to disappear, leaving only a fresh, clean, invigorating scent. If you have trouble memorizing the instructions, record part of this article for yourself, or buy Yogi Raj Alan Finger's "Life

Enhancing Meditations." With regular practice, you'll find it becomes natural and easy.

One client uses this technique so much, she's turned it into a verb! "So and so really got on my nerves today, so I satyam'ed for five minutes while he was talking to me. I can see I'll have to satyam some more because I can feel a little sadness clawing at my heart strings." She uses the meditation proactively, as a means to avoid latching onto negative emotions. Whether used for removing old grief or to prevent future attachments, sat yam offers a powerful way to keep moving forward. By embracing grief–literally inviting it into our hearts–we allow the energy of unconditional compassion to heal our wounds. Instead of dodging the emotions, we love them. As the saying goes, "If you love something, set it free." Love your grief, so that you CAN set it free!

Source: Laura Bruno is a Life Coach, Medical Intuitive, Animal Communicator and Reiki Master Teacher. She also teaches Conscious Eating 101 classes, Intuition workshops and Reiki Certification classes around the country.

Laura wrote the long-awaited book, "If I Only Had a Brain Injury: A TBI Survivor and Life Coach's Guide to Chronic Fatigue, Concussion, Lyme Disease, Migraine or Other "Medical Mystery", as well as The Lazy Raw Foodist's Guide, available at: **www.lazyrawfoodist.com**

Thank you, Laura and Yogiraj Alan.

Now, let's explore a more complex use of EFT. This technique is a little longer than what you have seen or used before. The beauty of this technique is that it keeps you tapping and talking and brings in lots of opportunities to genuinely "own" and acknowledge how you feel about what you are going through.

Special Note: The words shown below are shown for example, only. If different words resonate for you, please use your own words. You may say "this grief" or "this loss" or "I feel lost" or anything that <u>feels</u> right for you.

EFT for This Sadness and Loss

Tap on the Karate Chop point and say the sentences:

Karate Chop: Even though I feel this sadness and loss, I deeply and completely accept that I have these feelings.
Karate Chop: Even though I feel this sadness and loss, and I wish I could do something about them – whatever "something" is, and I deeply and completely accept that I have these feelings.
Karate Chop: Even though I feel this sadness and loss, I deeply and completely accept that I deserve to have these feelings because of all that it means.

Tap on each of the Tapping Points and say the sentence:

Top of Head: I feel this sadness and loss
Eyebrow: I feel this sadness and loss
Side of Eye: I feel this sadness and loss
Under Eye: I really feel this sadness and loss
Under nose: Sometimes I feel this sadness and loss and it's overwhelming
Chin: Sometimes I feel this sadness and loss and it makes me feel out of control

Collarbone: But I can't help but feel this sadness and loss
Underarm: I wish I could NOT feel this sadness and loss
Ribs: But I do feel this sadness and loss
Wrist: Yes, I feel this sadness and loss

Top of Head: I want to admit that I feel this sadness and loss
Eyebrow: I acknowledge that I feel this sadness and loss
Side of Eye: even if I don't like it
Under Eye: I still really feel this sadness and loss because I have every right
Under nose: But I wonder what it would be like NOT to feel this sadness and loss
Chin: But I don't know right now
Collarbone: because I still feel this sadness and loss
Underarm: But I would really like to not HAVE to feel this sadness and loss
Ribs: So someday I hope I can feel differently when I'm ready
Wrist: Yes, someday, when I'm ready

Take a deep breath and continue with another round:

Karate Chop: Even though I still feel this sadness and loss and I have lots of good reasons to feel this sadness and loss, I deeply and completely accept that I have these feelings, that I have the right to feel these feelings and that they are my feeling and that's OK... and maybe I can choose my feelings in the future instead of my feelings choosing me.
Karate Chop: Even though I have these remaining feelings of this sadness and loss which I deserve to feel - I know that deep down I really wish I could let go of all these feelings so I don't have to carry them around with me all the time and I completely and totally accept myself anyway.

Karate Chop: Even though I have these remaining feelings of this sadness and loss, I know that deep down I want to be a good person and don't need all this baggage, so I am proud of myself for wanting to let all this go but not until I am good and ready.

Tap on each of the Tapping Points and say the sentence:

Top of Head: I still feel this sadness and loss
Eyebrow: I still feel this sadness and loss
Side of Eye: I still have these remaining feelings that I feel this sadness and loss
Under Eye: I have many reasons to really feel this sadness and loss
Under nose: I am soon willing to let this go because I don't want it anymore
Chin: I know that when I feel this sadness and loss, it holds me back – and I want to let it go.
Collarbone: Even if I have to punish someone, it's not me I want to punish.
Underarm: I am open to learning how to let go of this sadness and loss
Ribs: I accept I feel this sadness and loss,
Wrist: I am now willing to let go of this and not have to feel my sadness and loss.

Top of Head: Even if I still feel this sadness and loss
Eyebrow: Even if I still don't understand
Side of Eye: And even if I don't feel like it's fair
Under Eye: I still really feel like not having to carry this around with me
Under nose: Even if I have lots of reasons, I'm tired of carrying this around with me
Chin: I know that when I feel this sadness and loss, it holds me back – and I want to finally let it go.
Collarbone: I have endured this long enough. I have survived and I am proud I have survived.
Underarm: I am open to learning how to let go of this sadness and loss
Ribs: I accept I feel this sadness and loss

Wrist: I am now willing to let go of this and FINALLY NOT have to feel this sadness and loss.
Top of Head: Even though I may feel I deserve to feel this sadness and loss
Eyebrow: Even if I deserve to feel this sadness and loss and have all these reasons to feel this sadness and loss
Side of Eye: I now can choose to let them go
Under Eye: I am happy I can let them go when I am ready.
Under nose: I have the right to choose NOT to feel this sadness and loss anymore.
Chin: I don't have to punish anyone right now and I can choose NOT to feel this sadness and loss anymore.
Collarbone: I can release this now when I feel like it.
Underarm: I have better things to do with all that emotion.
Ribs: Yes, I have better things to do with that emotion
Wrist: I am worthy of having a choice.

Take a deep breath and continue with another round:

Karate chop: Even though I have felt my sadness and loss for so long, I appreciate that I felt that because I was trying to protect myself somehow.
Karate chop: Even though I have felt my sadness and loss for so long, I appreciate that I had reasons to feel this sadness and loss.
Karate chop: Even though I used to feel my sadness and loss, I know that there is a better way and I appreciate that in me.

Tap on each of the Tapping Points and say the sentence:

Top of Head: The feeling of my sadness and loss is fading
Eyebrow: The feeling of my sadness and loss is starting to feel less troublesome
Side of Eye: I now can choose to let this go when I am ready.
Under Eye: I am worth the freedom that NOT feeling this anymore can give me.

Under nose: I now choose NOT to feel my sadness and loss anymore.
Chin: I know this used to be important to me and I am grateful that this somehow protected me
Collarbone: But it is time to move on and I can release this now
Underarm: I can release this now
Ribs: I have better things to do with all that emotion.
Wrist: Yes, better things to do

Top of Head: I am worthy of letting this go and I am happy I can finally let this go.
Eyebrow: I am safe to let this go when I am ready
Side of Eye: I now choose to let this go and feel safe
Under Eye: I am worth letting this go
Under nose: I now choose NOT to feel this sadness and loss anymore.
Chin: I choose not to feel this sadness and loss anymore
Collarbone: I am grateful I don't need this feeling any more
Underarm: I am grateful this feeling doesn't control me anymore and I choose to feel happy and free for letting this go
Ribs: I am happy to be free of this
Wrist: I feel happy and free and at peace

Take a deep breath and assess where you are. Tap more rounds, as necessary to bring you to a place of peace.

"I understand that grief is natural and I am letting it flow through me.
I am focusing on a future of love and acceptance and I know that it is okay to feel my feelings."
-Dr. Sue Lawton of doTERRA®

EFT for Depression

Focus in on this statement: "**I feel so depressed and hopeless about** _____ (insert your own situation i.e. not saying goodbye - getting angry - hurting someone - leaving or abandoning someone - saying or doing something - not doing something etc. And assess the level of your feeling, on a scale of 1 to 10.

10 = VERY INTENSE   and 1 = Not Very Depressed ___

Examples:

- Even though I'm tired of feeling so helpless...

- Even though I feel depressed about my life ...

- Even though I hate feeling hopeless . . .

- Even though I can't seem to get out of my house ...

- Even though I don't care about tomorrow

Round 1:

Tap the Karate Chop Point and say the sentence:

KC - Even though I'm tired of feeling so helpless...I deeply and completely love and accept myself.
KC - Even though this is an emotional burden for me... I accept myself and the feelings I have around this issue.
KC - Even though I know I am punishing myself with these feelings... I acknowledge and respect myself anyway.

Tap each of the 10 Tapping Points and Say the Phrase:

TH - This weighs heavy on my mind
EB - Sometimes it feels like a tight clamp around my body
SE - Especially when I think about it
UE - It's really hard to stop feeling depressed and helpless
UN - It makes me feel sad and disappointed in myself
CH - I feel like I need to carry this with me for a long time!
CB - It doesn't feel possible to let this go
UA - This is so heavy... and it's like a weight on my chest
Rib: This is really weighing me down
WR: And, with the weight of everything else going on, it is unbearable.

Take a deep breath... roll your shoulders, stretch, wiggle your toes. Assess the level of your feeling now: _____ (There is no right or wrong answer here.) The level may have gone down, stayed the same or maybe it even went up. It is not unusual for it to go up at this point. Just make note of how intense the statement "feels" to you after the first EFT tapping round.

Think about how it **FEELS**, because the intensity level of the statement of how depressed you **FEEL** will be more accurate if you plug into how it **FEELS** in your body, instead of what you **THINK** it is in your head.

Round 2:

Tap the Karate Chop Point and Say the sentence:

KC - Even though I've carrying this for while now... I love and accept myself anyway, and I forgive myself.
KC - Even though I don't know how to let this self blame go... maybe I'll find a way.
KC - Even though I think I **NEED** to hold onto this heavy feeling... I'm open to the possibility of letting it go

Tap each of the 10 Tapping Points and Say the Phrase:

TH - Part of me feels I **MUST** hold onto this
EB - And another part of me wants to let it go
SE - This heaviness has really stuck around
UE - I wonder if it's time to let it go?
UN - But if I let it go... I'll need to forgive myself...
CH - And I'm not sure I can forgive myself for this
CB - Maybe forgiving myself is more about realizing...
UA - that I did the best I could at that time
Rib-Yes, I did the best I could
WR-The best I could at that time

Take a deep breath... roll your shoulders, stretch your neck, wiggle your toes. How do you feel now, on a scale of 1 to 10? _____

Round 3: (No Setup) Just begin tapping . . .

Tap each of the 10 Tapping Points and Say the Phrase:

TH - It seems like I'm more open to forgiving myself about all of this
EB - It feels good thinking about being free of this weight!
SE - Do I need to be so hard on myself?
UE - Maybe I just need to give myself a bit of slack... and a whole lot of understanding
UN - I appreciate the new ways I am beginning to look at this
CH - I feel my mind and body getting a little lighter already
CB - I am relieved about the possibility of letting this go
UA - And that freeing myself of these heavy feelings...
Rib- May be surprisingly easy
WR-Yes, it may be easy to let these feelings go!

Take a deep breath . . . roll your shoulders, wiggle your toes. How do you feel now, on a scale of 1 to 10? _____

Remember, your goal is to get the intensity down to 1 or 2. Make sure you ask using the word **FEEL** instead of **think**. It's much easier to 'plug' into the issue when we are in our Heart. Asking "How do I feel?" helps you focus on feelings. Even slight shifts in your feelings can go a long way toward helping you make big changes in your life!

You can also take one of the other phrases shown at the top of the page "Tap and Talk" through your feelings.

Medical or Psychological Help

At some point, you may feel that you need to reach out to a medical doctor, a psychologist or psychiatrist. If so, please contact a trusted professional. Sometimes, this type of help is necessary in cases of extreme grief, depression or other feelings that do not respond to the energy clearing modalities described here.

Depression is a crippling disease that is hard to understand by those who have not experienced it. It can make you physically ill and mentally unstable. Depression can limit your personal growth, interfere with sleep patterns, eating habits, even personal hygiene. Many feel embarrassed and ashamed about the unwanted attention that being depressed can bring. Depression can also lead to feelings such as, "I hate myself and don't know why."

So, if you feel you need medical help, please contact your physician. Reach out to a friend if you are struggling and feel that additional support is what you need at this time.
If you are in relationship with a person who is showing signs of depression and you feel that person needs medical or psychological help, please take steps to get this help for your friend or loved one.

Mirror Work with EFT

EFT tapping can be even more powerful when done while looking at yourself in the mirror. Create a short phrase that captures how you are feeling and "Talk and Tap" by looking directly into the mirror. Use any of the scripts you've already seen or look at the next script in the section about Guilt.

Crystals and Essential Oils to Support You

Whether you diffuse one of these oils or create a rollerball and apply to your wrists or forearms, Frankincense and doTERRA®'s Joyful Blend and the Console Blend can support you as you feel your sadness. Another blend that may provide relief is doTERRA®'s Breathe Blend. Grief is often stored in the lungs and this blend will support your lungs as you cry and grieve and release your feelings of loss. A good way to use this blend is to put a few drops on cotton balls and inhale the aroma deep into your lungs. Repeat every few hours as needed.

Crystals that will support you include: yellow calcite and apache tear. Remember you can make a bracelet with beads of these stones (add clear quartz to amplify the properties of the other crystals) or buy small stones and carry in your pockets, purse or backpack.

Visitations and Dreams

Sometimes, we are visited by our loved ones who have crossed over. After my favorite aunt passed away, I dreamt that she and my grandmother were at the foot of my bed dancing. It was very real to me and I remarked the next day to my husband that I had been visited by the two of them. You may have very vivid dreams, during which you talk with or see the loved one for whom you are grieving. You may want to capture these dreams in your journal. It often helps to talk about these dreams with friends or trusted loved ones.

Guilt

Many times, guilt plays a large role in some of the depressing feelings that come up around grief and loss. Sometimes, we feel guilt or regret due to something we did to the person (or pet) who passed away. Sometimes, it is what we **didn't** do that causes us to feel guilty. You may even feel guilty about feelings you have, such as feeling relieved when the person passes after a long and painful illness. Here is an EFT script for releasing feelings of guilt.

EFT for Guilt

Focus in on this statement: **"I feel guilty about _____"** (insert your own situation, i.e., not saying goodbye - getting angry - hurting someone - abandoning someone - saying or doing something - not doing something etc.) Assess the level of your feeling, on a scale of 1 to 10.
10 = Feeling Extremely Guilty   1 = Feeling Not Guilty

Examples of "I feel guilty" sentences:

- "I feel terrible about not helping Mom when she needed me."

- "I feel guilty about not saying "I'm sorry" to Dad for what I said/did."

- "I feel responsible for _____ not working out like it should have with Jack.

Tap the Karate Chop Point and Say the sentence:

KC - Even though I feel sooooooo... guilty about _____
... I deeply and completely love and accept myself.

KC - Even though this is an emotional burden for me... I accept myself and the feelings I have around this issue.

KC - Even though I know I am punishing myself with these feelings... I acknowledge and respect myself anyway.

Tap each of the 10 Tapping Points and Say:

TH - This weighs heavy on my mind

EB - Sometimes it feels like a tight clamp around my body

SE - Especially when I think about it

UE - It's really hard to stop feeling guilty

UN - It makes me feel sad and disappointed in myself

CH - I feel like I need to carry this with me for a long time!

CB - It doesn't feel possible to let this go

UA - This is so heavy... and it's like a weight on my chest

Rib: This is really weighing me down

WR: And, with the weight of everything else going on, it is unbearable.

Take a deep breath and assess the level of your feelings now on a scale of 1 to 10 _____

(There is no right or wrong answer here.) The level may have gone down, stayed the same or maybe it even went up. (It is not unusual for it to go up at this point- please do not be alarmed.) Just make note of how intense the statement "feels" to you after the first EFT tapping round.

Focus on how you **FEEL,** because the intensity level of the statement of how guilty you **FEEL** will be more accurate if you plug into how it **FEELS** in your body, instead of what you THINK in your head.

Round 2:

Tap the Karate Chop Point and Say the sentence:

KC - Even though I've carrying this for a while now... I love and accept myself anyway, and I forgive myself.

KC - Even though I don't know how to let this self blame go... maybe I'll find a way.

KC - Even though I think I **NEED** to hold onto this heavy feeling... I'm open to the possibility of letting it go

Tap each of the 10 Tapping Points and Say:

TH - Part of me feels I **MUST** hold onto this

EB - And another part of me wants to let it go

SE - This heaviness has really stuck around

UE - I wonder if it's time to let it go?

UN - But if I let it go... I'll need to forgive myself...

CH - And I'm not sure I can forgive myself for this

CB - Maybe forgiving myself is more about realizing...

UA - that I did the best I could at that time

Rib-Yes, I did the best I could

WR-The best I could at that time

Take a deep breath... and ask yourself: How do I feel now, on a scale of 1 to 10? _____

Round 3: (No Setup – Just Tap)

Tap each of the 10 Tapping Points and Say:

TH - It seems like I'm more open to forgiving myself about this

EB - It feels good thinking about being free of this weight!

SE - Do I need to be so hard on myself?

UE - Maybe I just need to give myself a bit of slack... and a whole lot of understanding

UN - I appreciate the new ways I am beginning to look at this

CH - I feel my mind and body getting a little lighter already

CB - I am relieved about the possibility of letting this go

UA - And that freeing myself of these heavy feelings…

Rib- May be surprisingly easy

WR-Yes, it may be easy to let these feelings go!

Take a deep breath... roll your shoulders, stretch your neck, wiggle your fingers and toes. How do you feel now, on a scale of 1 to 10? _____

Remember, your goal is to get the intensity down to 1 or 2. Make sure you ask using the word **FEEL** instead of **think**. It's much harder to 'plug' into the issue when we are in our head. Asking "How do I feel?" helps you focus on feelings.

Even slight shifts in your feelings can go a long way toward helping you make big changes in your life!

And you may think of other forms of guilt, so tap on those, as well. Here are a few examples:

- "Even though I feel guilty about my mother's passing in the rest home......"

- "Even though I cry every day when I think about how he died alone....."

- "Even though I think I am a lousy lover/daughter/son/spouse...."

- "Even though I focus on what I did wrong and take no credit for helping him...."

- "Even though I'm not seeing things clearly....."

- "Even though I'm seeing this as a garage full of guilt instead of a launching pad for love...."

- "Even though this guilt is nothing more than a replay of the guilt trips my mother/father/sister/spouse laid on me...."

- "Even though I love to feel sorry for myself and don't know why....."

Dealing with complex emotional issues may require a more advanced form of tapping. If you are affected by ongoing negative emotions and feel you need help, please call me or another practitioner who can assist you with a session over the phone or in-person.

"When we are no longer able to change a situation, we are challenged to change ourselves."

-Viktor Frankl

Crystals and Essential Oils to Support You

For guilt, you can make a rollerball of doTERRA® Forgive Blend and apply to wrists. You can even apply around your belly button for more releasing and healing while you sleep. Other essential oils that help with guilt are Jasmine, Ylang Ylang, Neroli or Lavender. In fact, when you have no other oils, Lavender can be your "go to" essential oil for most emotional conditions. It is especially helpful when an emotion is preventing you from sleep. Rub your rollerball over the bottoms of your feet and toes and drift off to peaceful sleep.

Crystals can support you as you release the guilt and heal, and those that are most helpful are chrysocolla, peridot, larimar, malachite and rose quartz. In fact, Rose Quartz can be your "go to" crystal for just about any emotional concern.

Two or more of any crystal makes a grid. You do not have to have a fancy "grid framework" or multiple stones to create a grid. Your intention creates the grid and the function of the grid. So, take 2 or 3 of the stones listed, make a small grid and let the healing begin!

Ask your Angels to guide you to the best crystals for you and your journey of self-forgiveness for whatever it is for which you are feeling guilty.

Bitterness

Many times, after we begin to recover from a loss of any type, we may begin to remember bittersweet memories. Especially after a prolonged illness, there may be feelings of bitterness for time spent away from work or the affairs of day-to-day living. You may be left with expenses and duties for which you are not prepared.

As with the other feelings, allow yourself to feel what you feel. Use of the EFT scripts and "talk and tap" your feelings of bitterness away. Journaling may be very helpful, as well. Or, write a letter to your loved one and say everything that you want to say. See the section below on Anger for more ideas on letter writing.

Crystals and Essential Oils to Support You

For bitterness, use Bergomot, Roman Chamomile or doTERRA®'s Forgive Blend. You can diffuse or apply to wrists. I also like the Liquid Xanax recipe that I shared earlier.

Garnet, Blue Agate and Moss Agate are excellent crystals to help you heal and release bitterness. Blue Agate is helpful for those who are having a hard time with forgiveness and letting go of bitterness and resentments toward others.

Anger: What Do I Do Now?

As you begin to accept the reality of your loss, anger may come to visit. You may become angry at your loved one for leaving you. You may become angry at the way he/she treated you and about the future you will not enjoy with him/her. You may even become angry at God, doctors or hospitals or yourself.

Many feel that expressing anger is one of the signs that you are beginning to deal with the reality of your loss. When we don't express anger, we can become bitter and delay our recovery from grief. When we express anger inappropriately, we may hurt other family members and friends. You can choose to express your anger in appropriate ways and preserve or even improve relationships in your life.

If you are angry with your loved one for dying and leaving you, you can journal your feelings or write a letter. (See below for more information on letters.) You can also yell and scream or curse behind closed doors. Exercise is another way to let off steam and let feelings of anger escape in a healthy way. (Consult your doctor if you have any health concerns around exercise.)

It is important to express your feelings of anger in healthy ways that do not hurt you or another person and in ways that do not alienate you from the people in your life.

Ranting with EFT

Let's explore another really helpful EFT technique called EFT and Ranting. Ranting, Whining or Venting is a wonderful activity that provides an incredible energy release. It is very healthy and may serve to prevent alcohol abuse, panic attacks, road rage or other inappropriate behavior. And, when Ranting is paired with the stress release benefits of tapping with EFT, you will see results!

1. When you have about 15 minutes, with or without another person, sit down with an EFT Tapping Chart.

2. Think about something that really annoys you about your life and how it has changed with the passing of your loved one or friend.

(Please note we are not talking about major past issues of trauma and abuse in this case, but something you could really Vent about for ages and ages.)

Pick your topic, take a deep breath and start ranting.

Example. "Ok, about my mother. She REALLY gets on my nerves. Always bothering me,. checking up on me and interfering in my life. The other day, she actually _____."

3. As you **Rant,** you **Tap**. Start at the Top of the Head and travel down the body, ending with the Wrist. It is not necessary to say a Set Up Sentence with this method. Tap on all 10 Tapping Points, at least 5 to 7 X per point. Continue, as long as you have something to express. The tapping tends to get faster as you get into the Rant. That's all right and a natural response!

4. Continue to **Tap** and **Rant** until you:
   a) Run out of things to tap on
   b) Feel better
   c) Start laughing
   d) Have forgotten what you were tapping on!

Special note: It is not uncommon to begin a rant and feel a great deal of anger, which may be replaced by hurt or extreme sadness. If the tears come, know that you are accessing some very real feelings. You may want to reframe your session with a Set Up Sentence and tap a round or two on these new feelings.

And, remember, these feelings aren't really new. They may have been masked by your anger or other feelings related to your sense of loss.

Quick Coherence® Technique from Heart Math®

Create a coherent state in about a minute with the simple, but powerful steps of the Quick Coherence® Technique from Heart Math®. Using the power of your heart to balance thoughts and emotions, you can achieve energy, mental clarity and feel better fast anywhere. Use the Quick Coherence® Technique especially when you begin feeling a draining emotion such as frustration, irritation, anxiety or anger. Find a feeling of ease and inner harmony that's reflected in more balanced heart rhythms, facilitating brain function and more access to higher intelligence.

Step 1: Focus your attention in the area of the heart. Imagine your breath is flowing in and out of your heart or chest area, breathing a little slower and deeper than usual.

SUGGESTION: INHALE 5 SECONDS, EXHALE 5 SECONDS (OR WHATEVER RHYTHM IS COMFORTABLE)

Step 2: Make a sincere attempt to experience a re-generative feeling such as appreciation or care for someone or something in your life.

> *SUGGESTION: TRY TO RE-EXPERIENCE THE FEELING YOU HAVE FOR SOMEONE OR SOMETHING THAT YOU LOVE: A PERSON, A PET OR A SPECIAL PLACE.*

OR

> **FOCUS ON A FEELING OF CALM OR EASE.**

Source: www.heartmath.com

Letter Writing

Writing a letter to your loved one is one of the best ways to vent anger (or bitterness) and get out all of the feelings you may be experiencing around your sense of loss.

Writing a letter can be very healing, as old emotions, thoughts and baggage can be put into the letter. Don't edit or censure yourself. Let the words flow and be sure to capture everything you are feeling on the page or pages of the letter.

Some people write the letter and then hold a small ceremony and burn the letter in a fireplace or outdoor setting. You can also flush the letter or throw it away with your garbage. It is usually best to burn or destroy the letter, rather than keeping it among your possessions. Letting go of the letter serves as a type of "letting go" of the anger and grief and can be very healing for you.

Crystals and Essential Oils to Support You

For anger, use the Calming Blend by doTERRA® (also called Serenity) and Roman Chamomile. You can apply to the center of the chest and around the belly button. I also use the Liquid Xanax rollerball for anger and apply to pulse points on wrists. You can also diffuse any of these essential oils as you are writing your letters.

Angelite, Carnelian and Snowflake Obsidian are good crystals to help you with anger.

Using the essential oils and crystals for anger helps you feel your feelings and remain calm. Again, it's as if my angels are holding me in a loving embrace while I feel, release and heal the emotions that are coming up for me.

> *"I believe the hardest part of healing after you've lost someone you love, is to recover the 'you' that went away with them."*

- http://stayingaliveisnotenough.blogspot.com/

Fear: What Else Is Coming My Way?

Many times, a loss can open us up to worries and fears concerning our own mortality. Some people make use of this fear by making healthy choices regarding diet, exercise and other aspects of life that may prolong life or make the life we live more enjoyable.

Sometimes, there are fears around money, housing, career and other responsibilities that may change or be impacted by the death of a spouse, parent, child or life partner.

When it hits, nothing is more debilitating than fear. If it is left unchecked, fear can lead to panic, anxiety, insecurity and over time to hopelessness and depression.

EFT for Fear

Fear can be such a debilitating and disempowering emotion. It can strike without warning and hold you in its clutches for hours. How would you like a tool that will have you feeling your fear and then transforming it into a way to take action?

Here is a tapping script for fear that begins by addressing the genuine mood or feeling state you feel right now, then moves you into joy. (It makes use of 8 Tapping Points.)

Tap on Karate Chop Point and Say the sentence:

Even though I feel afraid right now, I deeply and completely love and accept myself.
Even though I'm afraid of many, many things, I accept who I am and how I feel...
Even though I'm frozen with fear right now, I accept how I feel and I deeply and completely love and accept myself.

Tap each of the 8 Tapping Points and Say:

EYEBROW: *I'm always afraid of what might happen*
SIDE OF EYE: *What if something else bad happens to me?*
UNDER EYE: *I feel the fear in my body*
UNDER NOSE: *I can feel the fear no matter what I do*
CHIN: *I feel worried and all alone*
COLLARBONE: *I'm afraid to let go of my fear*
UNDER ARM: *I feel afraid and petrified*
HEAD: *What if I can't let go of my fear?*

EYEBROW: *Yes, I'm focusing on the negative.*
SIDE OF EYE: *Maybe I don't want to be positive.*
UNDER EYE: *I feel afraid about so many things*
UNDER NOSE: *It's hard not to be fearful about my future*
CHIN: *I keep focusing on the negative.*
COLLARBONE: *I feel so overwhelmed.*
UNDER ARM: *It's hard to brave after what I've gone through*
HEAD: *I don't know if I want to be brave*

After you have used **EFT** to relieve the sensation of chronic fear in your mind AND your focus on the negative, you may give yourself permission to think about more positive thoughts:

Tap each of the 8 Tapping Points and Say:

EYEBROW: *I have decided to notice what is going right in my life*
SIDE OF EYE: *I'm ready to change my focus right now.*
UNDER EYE: *I choose to remember a time when I was brave*
UNDER NOSE: *I call upon my angels to help me heal daily*
CHIN: *I begin to look for miracles and courage in my life*
COLLARBONE: *I have so much to appreciate right now, and I look forward to more.*
UNDER ARM: *I appreciate who I am and how I feel today*
HEAD: *I appreciate people who love and support me*
EYEBROW: *I call upon my angels for courage*
SIDE OF EYE: *I admit that I am here and I am OK*
UNDER EYE: *I am alive and brave*
UNDER NOSE: *I love who I am and how I feel*
CHIN: *I'm grateful for beautiful memories of my courage*
COLLARBONE: *I appreciate my life and each new day*
UNDER ARM: *I'm grateful for peace and joy*
Head: *I love myself and I am brave*

Take a deep breath and then continue Tapping:

HEAD: *I love releasing my fear*
EYEBROW: *I love feeling brave*
SIDE OF EYE: *I appreciate feeling the courage inside me*
UNDER EYE: *I appreciate who I am and love myself*
UNDER NOSE: *I love my inner courage*
CHIN: *I appreciate all my feelings*
COLLARBONE: *I love myself and I'm OK*
UNDER ARM: *I'm grateful for this journey of courage*
       I am on.

*"COURAGE DOES NOT ALWAYS roar. Sometimes it is a quiet voice
at the end of the day, saying... 'I will try again tomorrow.'"*
-Mary Ann Radmacher

Communicate with Your Inner Guides and Angels

Your Angels and Inner Guides are always by your side. Everyone has one or more of these special messengers, who are helping you, guiding you every step of the way for every day of your life. Some people say we receive 70 to 80 hunches a day. Sometimes, it is a simple suggestion, such as "better take your umbrella." Often, it's "turn here, the address you want is on the left." Or, sometimes, you may hear, "don't trust what this person is saying."

In any event, these thoughts, feelings and other revelations are real guidance.

These special Spirit Beings love you very much and they will do anything within their power to help you and protect you. A Guide may remain with you for a lifetime, or one may come in and help you during a specific time, based upon your needs.

For example, your Angels and Guides may be helping you during this time of loss, whether you are aware of their special help or not.

The connection is usually telepathic, as in the little voice you hear in your head that you may think are your own thoughts. Often times they send you symbols, little flashes or movie clips or they may speak to you in dreams, or during your time in meditation. Many times, experiences are created to bring you into greater awareness of what is occurring in your life and to help you on your path.

Would you like to meet the wonderful energy who is sharing these inspirations? Would you like to learn how to call upon the help of your Inner Guides or Angels? Follow along with the "Meet Your Guide" meditation on my website: **www.soulrevelations.com**

Crystals and Essential Oils to Support You

For fear, use the Console Blend by doTERRA®, as well as Lavender, Marjoram, Bergamot, Neroli and Roman Chamomile. You can apply to the inside of the wrists and inhale 3 X after application. When the scent weakens during the day, reapply as necessary. You can also diffuse the Console Blend or Lavender for fear.

Lithium Quartz, Lepidolite (with its Lithium content) and Larimar are good crystals to have on hand for fear. Also, Black Obsidian is excellent. Carry or wear one of these crystals to soothe yourself as you release your fears.

"LARIMAR IS PARTICULARLY USEFUL FOR ALLEVIATING GUILT AND REMOVING FEAR. WHEN MOVING THROUGH PERIODS OF STRESS AND INEVITABLE CHANGE, IT ENABLES CHALLENGES TO BE MET WITH EQUANIMITY."
--JUDY HALL, THE CRYSTAL BIBLE, 2003

Lack of Trust

Sometimes after we have experienced the loss of a spouse, a job, a home or a pet, we experience a lack of trust. We may not trust God and may find our faith wavering. We may not trust others, and may begin to pull away from social interaction. We may not trust our own judgement, as irritability, frustration or agitation cloud our vision.

This is a great time to use EFT to "Vent and Tap" (see in the section on Disbelief and Shock) and work through the feelings that come up. Another helpful activity is to write a letter to God and share all of the feelings you have regarding your loss. Sometimes a visit with a trusted priest or pastor can also help to put into perspective your personal beliefs and how you might move on with the rest of your life.

Crystals and Essential Oils to Support You

During this time, Blue Chalcedony can be helpful in restoring trust. You might also reach for some of the angel crystals, such as Angelite or Celestite. Another crystal that may support you is Sugilite, which calls on Archangel Michael. He gives courage and protects you during this time of loss. Remember to get in touch with your own Inner Guides and Angels for support.

Essential Oils that may support you include the Console Blend by doTERRA® and Wild Orange. Diffuse one of these or create a Rollerball and apply to wrists and heart area to heal your lack of trust.

Physical Symptoms

Although most people think of grief as an emotional process, it often includes physical symptoms, as well. These can often include problems with insomnia, aches and pains, lethargy, weight gain/loss, immune system, nausea and other digestive concerns.

Please check in with your family physician if any of the physical problems last more than a few days. You may need some additional support to bridge the gap between now and your optimum state of wellbeing.

As I shared earlier, it is also important to eat a balanced diet, limit alcohol and follow your regular sleep and exercise schedule. There is a great tool in the Appendix called The Four Thumps and it comes from Energy Master Teacher Donna Eden. It is a daily routine that you can do to stimulate your immune system and bring your body back to its healthy state.

EFT is wonderful for physical ailments, as well as the emotional concerns. Here is a script that can be easily modified for just about any physical ailment. Refer to the EFT graphic and list of Tapping Points and complete directions in the beginning of the book.

EFT FOR PHYSICAL PAIN OR A PHYSICAL CONDITION OF ANY TYPE

Assess the level of your **PAIN,** on a scale of 1 to 10.
10 = Intense Pain   1 = Not very much Pain

Tap on Karate Chop Point and Say the sentence 3X:

Even though I have this Pain (toothache/allergy/cough), I deeply and completely love and accept myself and I forgive myself.

Tap each of the 10 Tapping Points and Say:

Pain in my _____ (right knee or whatever)

What is the number now? _____Describe the Pain: Does it have a color or texture? (i.e., sticky and gray in color) _____

Now, Tap on Karate Chop Point and Say 3X:

Even though I have this gray, sticky Pain hurting my right knee, I choose to drain it away.

Tap each of the 10 Tapping Points and Say:

Drain away (while imagining it draining away)

What is the number now? _____How has the color or texture changed? (i.e., thicker and darker in color) _____

Now, Tap on Karate Chop Point and Say 3X:

Even though I have this gray, sticky Pain hurting my right knee, I apply heat to it so that it becomes thinner and can drain away easily.

Tap each of the 10 Tapping Points and Say:

Apply heat to it (while imagining it being heated)

What is the number now? _____How has the color or texture changed? (i.e., thicker and darker in color)

_____

Take a deep breath and say "Peace" while holding one wrist with the opposite hand.

Other examples of Set-Up Phrases for Pain or Dis-ease:

Even though this pain is terrible, I don't want to change. I am used to it and don't want to let go.

Even though I think that only the painkiller can provide me relief from terrible pain, taking the homeopathic pills will prove to be equally effective for me.

Even though my inflexibility does not want me to change and be well, I deeply and completely love, forgive and accept myself.

Even though inflexibility has been staging this scary drama where I suffer a great deal of pain and I allowed myself to be conned by this play, i deeply and completely love, forgive and accept myself.

Even though my pain and suffering serve me in some way that I don't even understand, I deeply and completely love and accept myself.

Even though the doctors have told me this is terminal (inoperable, hopeless, etc), I deeply and completely love and accept myself.

Even though the doctors have told me this is hopeless, I choose to believe in the power of healing and have faith in a future for me.

Crystals and Essential Oils to support you

Essential Oils are a wonderful way to support your physical body for physical symptoms. Here are a few:

Insomnia: Liquid Ambien (20 drops of Lavender and 7 drops of Vetiver in a rollerball that is then filled to the top with coconut or almond oil), Lavender
Aches & Pains: Deep Blue Blend by doTERRA®
Lethargy/Fatigue: Basil, Eucalyptus, Geranium, Peppermint, Rosemary (remember my body wash with Rosemary and Peppermint? Perfect for Fatigue!)
Weight Gain: Slim & Sassy Blend by doTERRA®, Liquid Xanax
Weight Loss: Mandarin, Orange, Lemon, Ginger
Immune System: OnGuard by doTERRA®, Basil, Thyme, Frankincense
Nausea/Stomach/Digestive Issues: DigestZen Blend by doTERRA®, Ginger

Crystals that may support your physical symptoms:

Insomnia: Celestite, Lepidolite

Aches & Pains: Amethyst for headaches; Chrysocolla for joint pain; Moonstone for period pain; Rose Quartz for general aches and pains; Selenite for back pain

Lethargy/Fatigue: deep red crystals to bring in
energy; Apatite; Red Aventurine; Carnelian
Weight Gain: Boost your metabolism with Sun-
stone, Sodalite and Tiger Eye; add Rose Quartz
for self-love and Blue Lace Agate for the power
to say "No" to unhealthy food
Weight Loss: Lithium Quartz; Rose Quartz for self
love; Orange Kyanite
Immune System: Amethyst; Emerald; Lithium
Quartz
Nausea/Stomach/Digestive Issues: Amber- balances
the digestive system: Apatite- controls
digestion; Citrine- can balance the digestive
system; Blue Lace Agate-relieves gas pressure
in the intestines.

Remember to add Clear Quartz Crystals to amplify the
results of the crystals you select for your healing and
releasing work.

Acceptance: Moving On

At some point, the anger gives way, the depression clears
and you begin to accept your new life . . . a life without
your loved one, pet, friend or prior job.

Many people find that this new stage brings opportunities
for forgiveness. This type of forgiveness may include
forgiving the person who passed away, others in your
circle of family and friends and, in some cases, yourself.

"UNFORGIVENESS IS THE POISON YOU DRINK EVERY DAY,
HOPING THAT THE OTHER PERSON WILL DIE."
---DEBBIE FORD

*"As long as you don't forgive, who and whatever
it is will occupy rent-free space
in your mind." (or heart)*

--ISABELLE HOLLAND

EFT for Forgiveness

1. Forgive the offender for committing the act.

Tap on Karate Chop Point and Say the sentence 3X:

*Even though _____did _____, I
forgive him/her ... he/she was doing the best he/she could do.*

Tap each of the 10 Tapping Points and Say:

He hurt me (Example . . . use your own words)

Take a deep breath and continue.

2. Forgive the offender for the harm his act has caused
   you.

Tap on Karate Chop Point and Say the sentence 3X:

*Even though what happened has caused me problems for
_____years, that's ok, I forgive him/her.*

Tap each of the 10 Tapping Points and Say:

Caused problems for 15 years (Use your own words)

3. Forgive yourself for your reaction to the act.

Tap on Karate Chop Point and Say the sentence 3X:

Even though I _____,
that's okay, I was only reacting like most kids/people would. I
forgive myself for _____.

Tap each of the 10 Tapping Points and Say:

Hiding from people   OR

Refusing to make friends with any one
(Example...use your own words)

4. Forgive yourself for allowing your response to add to
the problem.

Tap on Karate Chop Point and Say the sentence 3X:

I forgive myself for allowing this _____ *to*
interfere with my enjoyment of life for the last ___*years. I've*
been doing the best I could do.

Tap each of the 10 Tapping Points and Say:

I forgive myself

(Example only. Saying something else may be better for
you)

Review how you feel. You may want to repeat one of the
quadrants that still has an emotional charge around it. Or,
just tap on new feelings that come up.

Source: Joleen Streit **http://www.hypnobirthing-nm.com/**

Ho'oponopono

Ho'oponopono is a Hawaiian term that means "to set right, to make right." Essentially, it means to make it right with the people with whom you have relationships. Some believe that the original purpose of Ho'oponopono was to correct the wrongs that had occurred in someone's life including errors, excesses and harm, even if the act was accidental.

Since the Hawaiian islands are small, compact communities, the people have a custom of setting things right before sunset or before the end of the day. If someone has hurt someone else with words or deeds, it is up to the two people to come together and forgive each other and "set it right."

For example, let's say your young son hits another child intentionally. When asked, the one who was hit would forgive the other immediately, because it is inappropriate to carry the feelings any longer than necessary. The other child reciprocates.

This is like a "Hawaiian Code of Forgiveness", and it's an important concept. Because, when we forgive others, we are also forgiving ourselves.

The current keeper of this code is a woman named MORRNAH NALAMAKU SIMEONA and IHALEAKALA HEW LEN, who is also known as Dr. Len. You can find a great deal of information on-line about the process of Ho'oponopono and Dr. Len.

This process is a wonderful way to forgive a loved one or friend who has crossed over and begin to feel healing almost immediately.

Basically, the Ho'oponopono steps to Forgiveness and Peace include:

1. Bring to mind anyone with whom you do not feel total alignment or support…anyone who evokes a negative memory, feeling or hesitation. In your mind's eye, construct a small stage that floats out in front of you.

2. Imagine an infinite source of love and healing flowing from a source above the top of your head. (this source of love and healing is your Higher Self.)   Just open up the top of your head,   and let the source of love and healing flow down, go inside your body, fill up the body, and see it overflow. Let it flow out of your heart and flow up to heal the person on the stage. Say "I love you."   Ask the person if they want to accept the healing. Remember everyone has Free Will . . . wait a few seconds.

   Say, "I'm sorry."

3. When you feel that the healing is complete, begin to talk with the person and   offer   your forgiveness   to   them, Say "I forgive you…" Next, ask them to forgive you.

   Say "Please forgive me"….

4. Next, let go of the person, and see them floating away. For a current, primary relationship, take some time to assimilate the relationship, and ask your healing angels to mend the relationship and set it up again with functional ties of unconditional love and understanding.

   Say "Thank you."

5. For a past relationship, cut the cord that connects the two of you totally and completely. Ask Archangel Michael to cut the cord or cords and heal you completely and effortlessly of the old hurts and dysfunctional patterns. You can envision Gabriel bringing in healing green light to heal the cuts.

6. Later, you may want to do this with every person in your life with whom you feel misaligned or where there may be friction or negative ties.

7. Remember: the final test is this: Can you see the person or think of him/her without feeling any negative emotions? If you do feel "charged," you may want to do the process again.

And you can do this process any time you like…in almost any situation…it only takes a few minutes.

Here's a way to combine EFT <u>and</u> Ho'oponopono:

EFT and Ho'oponopono

Bring to mind a relationship or situation for which you may want to use forgiveness.

Tap on Karate Chop Point and Say the sentence 3X:

Even though I have something within me that caused this situation, I deeply and completely love and accept myself and this opportunity to heal.

Tap on each of the 10 Tapping Points and Say:

TH: *Whatever is in me that brought this into my life*

EB: *I see that I brought this into my life*

SE: *I am sorry*

UE: *I forgive myself*

UN: *I forgive the other person*

CH: *I am grateful for this*

CB: *I allow myself to heal*

UA: *I love myself*

RIB: *I choose to expand this love to everyone involved*

WRIST: *I send peace and love to everyone involved*

Source: Modified slightly from an e-mail by Gwenn Bonnell, Master EFT Practitioner 4-22-09 **www.tapintoheaven.com**

Crystals and Essential Oils to Support You

Rhodonite, Rhodochrosite and Chrysoprase encourage forgiveness, whether it's forgiving others or yourself. Rose Quartz is another helpful crystal, as it supports Self-Love and love on all levels. Sugilite and Apache Tear also support forgiveness.

doTERRA® now has a blend called Forgive that is great for use when we being the heavy task of forgiveness. It can be diffused or made into a rollerball and applied to the wrists, heart area or collarbone, to support you while you do your forgiveness work.

Remember the Liquid Xanax, as well. This one can really hold you and support you as you do forgiveness work. If you don't have the Forgive blend, use Bergomot or Spruce and let the woodsy aroma of one of these essential oils lift your spirits.

SELF-FORGIVENESS EXERCISE with doTERRA® Essential Oils

Place 3 drops each of doTERRA® Essential Oils of Balance Blend® and Serenity Blend® in the palm of either hand. Rub directly around the belly button, while stating an affirmation and forming clockwise circles. Here is one idea for an affirmation: (Please adjust the verbiage to fit your situation.)

I forgive myself for believing misinformation about myself communicated by others. I forgive myself for denying my gifts and talents. I forgive myself for repeating destructive patterns and expecting a different outcome. I am free of criticizing, condemning, and judging myself. I release the past and live happily in the present.

Source: **Anna Casper, Reiki Master**
www.breathealittlemagic.com

Create a Vision for Your Life

About this time, you may be starting to feel better and you may be making plans for the rest of your life. Sometimes, it is helpful to use a template to guide you in creating a type of blue print for the life of your dreams.

One such template is called a "Living Vision." You can see a sample of one of these blueprints in the Appendix. Use this form and personalize it to match what you want to create. I used this form to find my husband, Steve, and to create my practice over ten years ago. It can be used for just about any aspect of your life.

EFT Choices Trio

Here is one of my favorite EFT scripts, which focuses on releasing the unpleasant feelings and integrating positive affirmations. With this EFT technique, you can replace negative feelings or habits with positive ones.

Assess the intensity of how you feel on a scale of 1 to 10, with 10 being the most intense feeling.____

1. Tap on Karate Chop Point and Say one of the sentences 3X or each of the sentences 1X:

Even though I feel a deep sense of loss and longing, I deeply and completely love and accept myself.

Even though I miss my loved one, I deeply and completely love and accept myself.

Even though I feel I'll never recover, I deeply and completely love and accept myself.

Tap each of the 10 Tapping Points and Say:

I miss my loved one (or say the NAME of your loved one)

Top of Head
Eyebrow
Side of Eye
Under Eye
Under Nose

Chin
Collarbone
Under Arm
Under Rib
Wrist

Take a deep breath and continue.

2. Tap on each of the 10 Tapping Points and Say

I choose to release this sense of loss (or your positive choice)

Top of Head
Eyebrow
Side of Eye
Under Eye
Under Nose
Chin
Collarbone
Under Arm
Under Rib
Wrist

Take a deep breath and continue.

3. Tap on each of the 10 Tapping Points and alternate the sentences, as shown here. (Use your own words)

Top of head: *I miss my loved one (Say the name if you want)*
Eyebrow: *I choose to release this sense of loss*
Side of Eye: *I miss my loved one*
Under Eye: *I choose to release this sense of loss*
Under Nose: *I miss my loved one*
Chin: *I choose to release this sense of loss*
Collarbone: *I miss my loved one*
Under Arm: *I choose to release this sense of loss*

Under Rib: *I miss my loved one*
Wrist: *I choose to release this sense of loss*

Remember to END with the Positive Choice statement.

Source: Dr. Patricia Carrington
www.emofree.com/articles-ideas/professional/choices-article.html

EFT Alternate Tapping Plan

This one looks simple, and it is, but don't let its simplicity fool you: It is Powerful! Before you begin, think of a peaceful time or a peaceful place in your past.

Now, focus on the situation, emotional issue or physical condition that is troubling you around your recent loss.

Assess the intensity of your feeling on a scale of 1 to 10 10= very intense   1= not at all _____

Focus on this feeling of _____ and
1. Begin tapping on the middle of your forehead and say: *I release and let go all of the sadness of my feeling of*

   _____

2. Begin tapping on the side of your eye and say: *I release and let go all of the fears of my feeling of*

   _____

3. Begin tapping under your eye and say: *I release and let go all of the emotional traumas of my feeling of*

   _____

4. Begin tapping on your collarbone and say: *I release and let go all of the helplessness, hopelessness, stress and anxiety and know that it's truly safe to let it go.*

5. Encircle the wrist on your non-dominant hand with your dominant hand and take a deep breath, while saying: *Peace. . .*

Now, envision or remember that peaceful time or place in your life and take yourself there . . . now. . .

Source: Robert G. Smith **www.fastereft.com** Used with permission

Self-Love Tool

Feeling scared, anxious or struggling?
Step #1: Expand your energy out
Step #2: Go into your heart
         Put your hand over your heart
Step #3: Take 3 deep breaths
Step #4: Say "I Love You" 3 X
         Say "You Are Safe" 3 X
With practice, you will be able to:
Expand, Hand on Heart, Breathe, Say "I Love You" 3X-- all in a few seconds!

Source: Matt Kahn video www.truedivinenature.com

What's Next?

The Rest of Your Life . . .

You have been very brave, patient and steadfast in opening to your pain, your feelings of aloneness and your tears. You have cried and laughed and experienced many things over the time since you started this book. One of the bits of encouragement I want to give you as the book closes is this:

Be gentle with yourself. Be good to yourself. Be honest with yourself.

You have opened yourself to many new ways of feeling, thinking and acting. Some part of everyday will be spent using some of the tools and techniques you have learned within these pages or from other books, friends, websites and sources of information, wisdom and comfort.

Please, let this search continue. For as you search for the truth in your life, you will find hope, joy and everything you desire. As you open to honesty and seek relationships with other people, you will probably surprise yourself with how you will change and grow.

Do I use EFT every day? Yes, in some way. Do I meditate every day? Most days. Do I journal every day? Several times a week.

I use these tools because it helps me plug into who I really am, into my source of joy and wholeness. It's like taking a shower or brushing my teeth: these activities have become a part of my life. Like brushing my teeth, I see the benefits when I use the tool and what happens when I don't!

Also, I read books and enjoy on-line guides and information, watch movies and DVDs on a wide range of topics. All of these activities help me navigate life, grow spiritually and learn more about myself and other people. This thirst for knowledge supports me in lots of ways and I never tire of learning new things.

Another thing I did after my second divorce was to revisit a creative hobby that I enjoyed when I was younger: photography. I love to take photos with my camera and phone and create photo gifts, photo books and other artistic photo projects. By tapping into something I enjoyed when I was younger, I was able to heal myself and move on.

What did you enjoy when you were a child or young adult that you could revisit now?

Visit a Psychic Medium

It may be helpful for you to meet with a psychic medium, who can connect with your loved one who has crossed over. Most mediums recommend that you wait at least 6 months before asking for messages from your loved one. This period of time allows you to begin the grieving process and begin to move through the emotions that accompany such a loss.

You will want to ask friends or family members for referrals to a reputable medium. My husband Steve and I are mediums. We also know a number of reputable mediums in the DFW area to whom we can refer you.

Please review some tips about "sitting for a medium" so you will be ready for your meeting. You will see these in the Appendix.

The most important thing to remember is that you do not want to volunteer information about your loved one or the manner in which he/she passed. Allow the medium to connect with your loved one and bring through messages or evidence that you can validate, so that you know that the information is coming from your loved one on the other side.

A Course in Miracles

I'd like to close with a lesson from <u>A Course in Miracles</u>, a wonderful collection of lessons and information, which integrates ideas from Christianity, Eastern religions, mysticism, psychology, and Platonism. ACIM presents a view of reality as consisting of a single thing, the love of God and the physical world as a projection in the mind. ACIM focuses on cultivating awareness of love in the self and in others. Believers in ACIM consider it an inspired scripture that also possesses a greater sense of truth. It was channeled or received from Spirit from a woman named Helen, who recorded it in 1975 and made it available to the world. You will find a number of on-line sites that offer the lessons free of charge. Some sites even offer an audio recording of the lessons for free.

You can also find your own copy of ACIM at any bookstore, used bookstore or on Ebay or Amazon.com.

This lesson may seem a little strange to you, because it is Lesson 41, not Lesson 1, yet it may speak to you today. (Each lesson builds on the one prior to it and takes you, with tiny, baby steps, toward a knowledge of God's love that is unlike anything you might have learned in any church or synagogue.)

Lesson 41 - Course in Miracles

Today's idea: "God goes with me wherever I go."

"Today's idea will eventually overcome completely the sense of loneliness and abandonment all the separated ones experience. Depression is an inevitable consequence of separation. So are anxiety, worry, a deep sense of helplessness, misery, suffering and intense fear of loss.

The separated ones have invented many "cures" for what they believe to be "the ills of the world." But the one thing they do not do is to question the reality of the problem. Yet its effects cannot be cured because the problem is not real. The idea for today has the power to end all this foolishness forever. And foolishness it is, despite the serious and tragic forms it may take.

Deep within you is everything that is perfect, ready to radiate through you and out into the world. It will cure all sorrow and pain and fear and loss because it will heal the mind that thought these things were real, and suffered out of its allegiance to them.

You can never be deprived of your perfect holiness because its Source goes with you wherever you go. You can never suffer because the Source of all joy goes with you wherever you go. You can never be alone because the Source of all life goes with you wherever you go. Nothing can destroy your peace of mind because God goes with you wherever you go.

We understand that you do not believe all this. How could you, when the truth is hidden deep within, under a heavy cloud of insane thoughts, dense and obscuring, yet representing all you see? Today we will make our first real attempt to get past this dark and heavy cloud, and to go through it to the light beyond.

. . . In the morning, as soon as you get up if possible, sit quietly for some three to five minutes, with your eyes closed. At the beginning of the practice period, repeat today's idea very slowly. Then make no effort to think of anything. Try, instead, to get a sense of turning inward, past all the idle thoughts of the world. Try to enter very deeply into your own mind, keeping it clear of any thoughts that might divert your attention.

From time to time, you may repeat the idea if you find it helpful. But most of all, try to sink down and inward, away from the world and all the foolish thoughts of the world. You are trying to reach past all these things. You are trying to leave appearances and approach reality.

It is quite possible to reach God. In fact it is very easy, because it is the most natural thing in the world. You might even say it is the only natural thing in the world. The way will open, if you believe that it is possible. This exercise can bring very startling results even the first time it is attempted, and sooner or later it is always successful. We will go into more detail about this kind of practice as we go along. But it will never fail completely, and instant success is possible.

Throughout the day use today's idea often, repeating it very slowly, preferably with eyes closed. Think of what you are saying; what the words mean. Concentrate on the holiness that they imply about you; on the unfailing companionship that is yours; on the complete protection that surrounds you.

You can indeed afford to laugh at fear thoughts, remembering that God goes with you wherever you go."

Source: Course in Miracles, Lesson 41, by Dr. Helen Schucman and Dr. William Thetford ©1975

Section Three – Tools & Techniques

The Four Thumps

In an Energy Slump? Use this routine to RECHARGE your batteries, JUMP START your energies, ACTIVATE your immune system, BOOST your metabolism, and DETOX naturally. This reminder from Gwenn Bonnell is part of Donna Eden's Energy Medicine techniques. It's a must in your self-care daily routine. Use it first thing in the morning, and anytime you feel your energy slump!

THE FOUR THUMPS

Perform daily to boost your immune system, increase your strength & vitality, ground your energy, and support your natural rhythm.

#4: Under Eye Points (Cheekbones)

#1: Cross Hands, Thump K-27 Points

#2: Thymus Point

#3: Spleen Neurolymphatic Points

For each step, tap or thump the points while breathing in through the nose & out through the mouth for about 20 seconds.

© Copyright All Rights Reserved 2009 Gwenn Bonnell

Graphic used with permission. **www.tapintoheaven.com**

Step 1: RECHARGE YOUR ENERGY by Tapping Under Each Eye

Tapping under the center of each eye on the cheekbone stimulates acupoints on the Stomach Meridian. This meridian, or energy pathway, travels down body and off the 2nd toe. By tapping under the eye, you are connecting with the earth's energies – something we do less and less of as we get more and more into the technical age.

This is the ultimate in green energy because it helps you plug your electrical body into the earth's magnetic energy. It's literally recharging your batteries. Think of when you feel the most balanced, grounded and nurtured and I bet it's remembering an experience you had out in nature. A picnic in the park, hiking in the mountain or feeling the sand under your toes at the beach.

It's important to spend time outdoors every day – and to use these tapping points to connect with the earth's energies.

STEP 2: JUMPSTART YOUR SYSTEM by Tapping Under the Collarbone

Find these points at the end of the Kidney Meridian by finding where the head of the collarbone protrudes on either side of your throat. Bring your fingertips down a bit below the bone and out to either side. You'll feel a dip between the collarbone (clavicle) and breastplate (sternum). That's where you want to tap or massage.

Thumping or deeply massaging these points under the collarbone jumpstarts your system by getting the energy moving forward through ALL the meridians. If you find it a struggle to put one foot in front of the other, you know you REALLY need this! Thumping these points on a daily basis will stop you from ever getting to that point!

The more you stimulate these points, the more healing energy your body can access. Not only do these points clear the chest cavity and open up respiration, they also counteract stress and balance the thyroid. So get thumping!

STEP #3: A QUICK ENERGY BOOST by Thumping the Center of the Chest

Think Tarzan and the Apes and do the Tarzan Thump! The Thymus is a long, skinny gland in the center of your chest and is responsible for boosting the T-cells in your immune system. When you're sick, the Thymus shrinks, and if it's totally shriveled you're probably dead. So you can't stimulate this enough!

A great affirmation to repeat as you thump the Thymus is: *"My life energy is high! I am full of love! I have love, faith, trust, gratitude and courage."*

STEP #4: BOOST YOUR METABOLISM by Massaging Between The Ribs

These points under the breast between the 7th & 8th ribs are known as the "Spleen Neurolymphatic Points" and help metabolize food, release toxins, boost your immune system and balance blood chemistry and electrolytes.

If these points are sore, massage them for a few days to release toxic build-up so thumping isn't so painful.

The effects of massaging the spleen Neurolymphatic Points make the Four Energy Thumps a must-do around mealtime, especially if you're feeling sluggish or tired after you eat!

WHEN TO DO THE FOUR ENERGY THUMPS

Try this routine first thing in the morning to get your day started on a positive note. This is a wonderful self-care routine anytime during the day you need an energetic pick-me-up, especially around mealtime. I'll caution you, however: **DO NOT DO** the Thymus Thump before retiring for the night (speaking from experience LOL).

Source: Gwenn Bonnell www.tapintoheaven.com

You may also want to go to YouTube and search for **Donna Eden's 5 Minute Energy Routine.** There are several videos, and I don't know why, but all of them are slightly over 5 minutes!

However, with a little practice, you can easily do the routine in 5 minutes or less. It is a great way to start your day.

Then, about 2 or 3 o'clock, when your energy is starting to flag, do the 4 Thumps and get yourself going again. This time, without caffeine or sweets!

Create a Living Vision for Your Life

Think about what you most want for your life. Use this as a type of template. You can retype this and add in all of the elements to make it your own. Or, you can start from scratch.

I see myself enjoying all of the camaraderie, challenges and a creative outlet, working with the other employees. (or as an entrepreneur) I see myself working as a _____(position) with _____ (type of company) in _____ (city) doing_____(job description) and making the most of my skills, abilities and talents. (It is important NOT to mention a particular company, group, etc., unless that is a VERY SPECIFIC goal of yours, say to work for Google or Microsoft, etc. When you limit yourself to just one or two companies, you limit the Universe and what it can deliver to you.) I work with fun, smart, nice, organized and focused people, who appreciate me and the skills and talents I bring to the job place every day.

I see educational opportunities, travel opportunities and career advancement options, as well, all of which keep me interested, challenged and _____.
(add adjectives which make this YOUR experience)

I see myself enjoying my new city (or a specific city in your metropolitan area) with my apartment/home just a short drive/commute from my job. I also enjoy the wonderful shopping, cultural and educational opportunities nearby, and I see myself enjoying all of the items that help support me in my wonderful life.

I see myself checking my bank account on-line and surveying a recent deposit of my pay of $_____ per each two wee pay period. My benefits package is extremely generous, with a wonderful medical, dental and vision plan, 401K, expense account and many other perks, all of which I deserve and find very appealing.

And (if in a significant relationship or desiring one):
I see myself walking in a beautiful park, enjoying myself with my _____ (spouse/life partner/children/pet/s), loving life and being open to new opportunities to meet people. My social life is happy and full, with activities with single friends and other couples, who enrich our lives with new ideas, new philosophies and new chances for personal growth. My relationship with my spouse/partner is rich and fulfilling...we have excellent communication skills, regular "date" nights and a satisfying physical relationship. He/she truly is "my best friend." (Enhance to add all types of activities you enjoy, both with and without your partner.)

All in all, I have a wonderful life. It is rich, full and meaningful for me every day in every way. I am so blessed and grateful for this life and the ease with which I navigate my path.

Note: If you are looking for a mate, make a list of about 35 things you are looking for and be careful not to have any certain person in mind. That way, if it works out with a person you know, it was meant to be. If it doesn't work out and you meet someone new, then THAT person is the person for you, based upon your "Wish List."

This can be personalized in so many ways.....depending upon your personal goals. It can be tailored to finding the perfect home, job, mate, second home....you get the idea. Make it uniquely yours! Keep everything in PRESENT TENSE.

Sitting for a Medium

By either attending a medium's gallery, circle of light or séance or a private reading there are certain guidelines the sitter should follow to get the most out of a reading. First and foremost you should have an open mind. Skeptics are welcome! You should always be skeptical to make sure you get an accurate message that you or someone you know can validate. But if you go into a circle with your arms crossed and the attitude that the medium is going to "have to prove to me" or if a certain individual doesn't come through for you, then you won't be a believer, then it isn't going to happen. You will find out soon enough when you cross over yourself. I love it when mediums bring through a spirit that was an atheist in their earth life. And the first message to the sitter is, "I was wrong!"

When the medium delivers a message you should only validate it with a "yes" or "no." After the reading you can put the pieces together and explain to the medium who they were talking to. You also want to give the medium a chance to give as much information as they can. If the medium tells the sitter that they have a father figure coming though, and you answer, "That's my father Bob!" then you have prevented the opportunity for the medium to tell you that the spirit is "Bob." If you have a question to ask, ask the spirit to which the medium is communicating with to give you an answer. Be a skeptic! Make those on the other side and the medium work for you. Remember you want indisputable proof! Before John Edward's mother died of cancer, he and his mother agreed on three "code" words that she could give to another medium to prove she had crossed over and was well. It took John Edward nearly three years to hear all of the code words from his mother.

The great magician Harry Houdini also had a similar arrangement with his wife and he never did receive validation after her crossing. You have to be open-minded; as spirit will give you the messages you need to know at this time and place in your life. Don't let the medium ask you questions! Ask the medium what they are seeing and if that makes sense to you. Validate it by saying, "Yes, that makes sense to me." And have them go on. Remember the medium doesn't have to understand the connections, just you do!

It is the medium's job to provide or share everything they are hearing or seeing for you, and your job to record and open your mind up to think of all of the possibilities and facts that are brought through so you can validate them now or later. Some mediums may get a full name, while others may be a bit more general. If a medium brings through a grandmother spirit but can't give you a name, you don't want to dismiss the message. Let the medium describe what she looks like, where she lives, a past event you and your grandmother shared. This way you can validate the message.

Remember a medium is like a radio and sometimes the signal they are receiving on the other side is weak or distorted. You don't want to dismiss a message coming through to you from a grandfather that the medium says is a "Jack," if you called him "Jackson." If a medium is giving you a message that you don't understand at the moment, just say, "I can't validate that right now." Don't keep saying "no, no, no," to the medium because the person on the other side will give up and the medium will give up. Two days later you may contact the medium and say, "Oh, I did have an Uncle Ted. What was the message?" but, then it's too late.

Record or ask someone else to write down everything the medium is saying. You can go back over the notes or the recording later to validate something the medium said. During the reading you want to give the medium your undivided attention. Stay present. Your loved ones only have so much time to connect because it takes so much energy to communicate.

Know your family history before you sit with a medium. I have had great-grand parents come through whom I never met. They were able to tell the medium everything I was currently involved in, were I worked and things that were coming up in the near future! And they were right on! If I would have dismissed them or failed to validate them, I would have missed some important messages.

Sometimes those who have been on the other side the longest have stronger voices or have an easier time contacting us. On the flip side of this, don't discount messages of recently deceased loved ones. I have brought through messages from a man who had crossed over just eight days earlier and several just a few months earlier. So leave your mind open as to who may show up.

Spirits will give names of friends and loved ones still living to get your attention and to prove that they see what is going on in your life now! I call these a "shout out!"

Some of the best and strongest validations have come from information the sitter was unaware of, and by checking with someone else in his family, he found the message to be true. This is further validation that the medium isn't reading your mind. In some cases your relatives on the other side may give you information about something that is going to happen in the near future for you to validate later.

Source: Steve Spur, **www.cowboypsychic.com**, © 2008

Bibliography

Aroma Tools, <u>Modern Essentials</u>, 6th Edition, 2014
Bodine, Echo, <u>Echoes of the Soul</u>, 1999
Conner, Janet, <u>Writing Down Your</u> Soul, 2009
Church, Dawson, <u>The EFT Manual</u>, 2013
Diamond, Christi Turley, <u>Aroma Heal</u>, 2014
DuBois, Allison, <u>We Are Their Heaven</u>, 2007
Edward, John, <u>One Last Time</u>, 1999
Eden, Donna, <u>Energy Medicine</u>, 2008
Eppler, LaRue and Vanessa Wesley, <u>Your Essential Whisper</u>, 2008
Gerber, Dr. Richard, <u>Vibrational Medicine</u>, 2001
Goff, Adrienne, <u>Crystal Healing for the Whole Being</u>, 2011
Hall, Judy, <u>The Crystal Bible</u>, 2003
Hartman, Silvia, <u>Energy EFT</u>, 2014
Kubler-Ross, Elizabeth, <u>On Death and Dying</u>, 1969
Lawton, Dr. Sue and Rebeca Linder Hintze, <u>Living Healthy and Happily Ever After</u>, 2014
Newton, Michael, <u>Journey of Souls</u>,1994
Newton, Michael, <u>Destiny of Souls</u>, 2000
Permutt, Philip, <u>The Crystal Healer</u>, 2007
Raphaell, Katrina, <u>Crystal Healing, Vol 2</u>, 1987
Raphaell, Katrina, <u>Crystal Enlightenment, Vol 1</u>, 1985
Schwartz, Robert, <u>Your Soul's Plan</u>, 2009
Spur, Steve, <u>Crossroads</u>, 2013

You may also visit my website and see what I am currently reading. I post each book I read throughout the year on my site: www.soulrevelations.com

About the Author

As a spiritual mentor, PJ Spur utilizes many different resources and healing modalities in her practice, where she supports people who are "awakening" to their spiritual journey. With a specialty in past life regression and life-between-lives journeys, PJ is a Certified Hypnotist, a Medium and an Angel Certified Practitioner.

In 2008, PJ was led to write an e-book on grief and lead a series of classes for grieving people. In 2015, PJ began updating the book for publication with new information, including new healing tools and ways to use crystals and essential oils for grief support. The book is entitled "Navigating Grief with Grace."

PJ shines a light, so you can see your way to healing and transforming your own life. www.soulrevelations.com

With her husband, Steve Spur, PJ also teaches classes in psychic and mediumship development, how to meet your spirit guides and other classes that help people navigate their lives with more joy and peace. Their Soul Compass Meetup features classes and events each month. www.meetup.com/soul-compass

Special Note from PJ Spur: The services I provide are those of a mentor or type of guide for spiritual and personal transformation and growth. I may reference hypnosis, EFT, Reiki or any number of other energy clearing modalities. I do not represent my services as any form of health care or psychotherapy. I am not a healer nor a medical professional. I am here to help you remember who you are at a soul level, in order to achieve your optimum level of well-being.

www.ingramcontent.com/pod-product-compliance
Lightning Source LLC
Chambersburg PA
CBHW060949040426
42445CB00011B/1072